THE HONORS THESIS

A Handbook for Honors Directors, Deans, and Faculty Advisors

This volume is dedicated to our friend and editor
Jeff Portnoy, for his encouragement, good humor,
support, and endless patience.

—*Mark Anderson, Karen Lyons, and Norman Weiner*
1 November 2014

THE HONORS THESIS

A Handbook for Honors Directors, Deans, and Faculty Advisors

by Mark Anderson, Karen Lyons, and Norman Weiner

Series Editor | Jeffrey A. Portnoy
Georgia Perimeter College

National Collegiate Honors Council
Monograph Series

Manufactured in the United States

National Collegiate Honors Council
1100 Neihardt Residence Center
University of Nebraska-Lincoln
540 N. 16th Street
Lincoln, NE 68588-0627
www.ncnchonors.org

Production Editors | Cliff Jefferson and Mitch Pruitt
Wake Up Graphics LLC

Cover and Text Design | 47 Journals LLC

International Standard Book Number
978-0-9825207-0-3

TABLE OF CONTENTS

INTRODUCTION

Writing the honors thesis is arguably the most rewarding undertaking of a student's undergraduate educational experience, the capstone for honors work as well as undergraduate studies. A thesis or creative project in a discipline introduces students to the world of scholarship and professional activity in a way that no single course, either semester-long or even year-long, can. In-depth work—whether a laboratory experiment, as it might be in the sciences; hands-on research or experience, as it might be in the social sciences or pre-professional fields; intensive analysis unearthing ideas or following new lines of thought, as it might be in the humanities; a creative performance or exhibition, as it might be in the arts; or an interdisciplinary exploration of a topic that brings together a number of fields—means that students' original ideas and critical thinking can lead them to new paths of knowledge and understanding. This experience is why some honors educators consider honors thesis work to be the essence of an honors education, and why, in many departments and at many institutions, the honors thesis, rather than honors courses, truly defines the honors experience.

For many students, the value of the thesis is located not just in the product, the thesis itself, but also in the thesis process. Many cherish the personal relationship they develop with their thesis advisor and appreciate the many ways, from conceptualizing and structuring thesis work to establishing interim goals and deadlines, that their faculty mentors helped them during the thesis process. Students typically discuss the ways in which their thesis work deepened and enriched their understanding of a specific topic, but they are equally outspoken about the personal value of the process; the ways their thesis work gave them an insight into their own abilities; how they learned to overcome obstacles, setbacks, and limited resources; the importance of time management; and the necessity for constantly honing their thinking and writing skills.

In the basic faculty advisor/student relationship for thesis work, we find both the paradigm for advanced independent student work and the model for faculty mentoring and structuring this process. This handbook is intended to enlarge the scope of that paradigm to assist honors programs and colleges in creating and structuring manageable, rewarding, and worthwhile experiences for everyone involved.

WHY A HANDBOOK FOR HONORS DIRECTORS, DEANS, AND FACULTY ADVISORS?

There is a great deal of honors thesis information out there. Every college bookstore stocks guides for students who are writing research papers. New books on research methods and thesis writing appear frequently, with some specifically oriented to the undergraduate thesis. And many of these are indeed helpful to students who are planning for or working on their honors thesis. For example, Charles Lipson's excellent *How to Write a BA Thesis* (2005) currently seems to be the most popular student guide for the honors thesis; it is a required or recommended text in scores of honors programs and colleges across the United States.

In addition, almost every honors program and college generates a great deal of information and advice about the thesis. Typically they publish an institutionally specific set of guidelines for the thesis covering the rationale, local requirements and forms, deadlines, advice on the best ways to approach the thesis, summaries of typical or unique projects, and even profiles of successful students. These local materials may be distributed to students and others as a series of handouts, included as a section in the college or program's Honors Handbook, or made available as web pages on the local honors website. In fact, most established honors colleges and programs use all of these methods for distributing thesis information. These materials provide important and easily accessible information for the students planning or already engaged in their thesis work and for the faculty who are directing thesis students.

None of these thesis materials, however, are aimed at honors deans, directors, faculty, or staff. But why should they be? After all, they run honors colleges and programs and perhaps even designed them. They are already the experts: they have written their own thesis, they are familiar with the conventional advice about writing a thesis, and they have a broad understanding of the common problems and pitfalls students may encounter during their thesis work. Moreover, why should they try to fix what is not broken? Many administrators have inherited a workable thesis structure from their predecessors; they have made adjustments where necessary or rewritten some of the materials and forms.

Because the educational landscape, including new technologies, service learning, and alternative pedagogies, has changed so dramatically and created new thesis possibilities as well as problems, some directors and deans may not have had the opportunity to consider fully the ramifications of offering and supporting thesis work. With the rapid growth in the number of honors programs and colleges in the last two decades, and with similar changes in the educational environment—the digital revolution, the expansion of student internships and foreign study, and the inclusion of such fields as business and engineering in honors work, many honors directors and deans have asked the National Collegiate Honors Council (NCHC) for a publication that would assist them in integrating the honors thesis into the current educational context.

For this handbook, we have drawn on the philosophies and practices for the honors thesis at a wide variety of NCHC member institutions. In addition, we have benefited greatly from the wide range of experiences of honors deans and directors across the nation. This handbook is intended to help all those who design, administer, and implement honors thesis programs—honors directors, deans, staff, faculty, and advisors—evaluate their thesis programs, solve pressing problems, select more effective requirements or procedures, or introduce an entirely new thesis program. Our goal is to provide everyone involved in honors thesis projects with a range of options, models, and best practices for promoting superior thesis work and justifying to students, to faculty, and to administrators the real value of the honors thesis, as well as the commitment and costs it requires at every level.

This handbook focuses on the place of the thesis in an honors college or program. We will consider why many honors programs and colleges require every honors program or college student to produce an honors thesis and why some do not. We will discuss what honors directors and deans see as the value of a thesis for students, for faculty, for their honors program or colleges, and for their college or university. We will explore what might constitute an honors thesis, including traditional research, a creative project in the arts, a pre-professional project, interdisciplinary or collaborative projects, and what some faculty in Education refer to as "action research." (See, for example, Sagor, 2000.) This monograph will also address how honors directors and deans distinguish an honors thesis from such programmatic elements as independent study courses and other faculty-student research projects. We will examine the advantages and disadvantages of a range of options for an honors thesis program; practical strategies for helping students understand the value and viability of the thesis and for convincing faculty that advising a thesis is worth their time and energy; and solutions to common thesis problems, such as helping students finish on time, improving the percentage of students who complete the thesis, and rewarding faculty for their work. One basic question undergirds this enterprise: within a specific academic environment, how can an honors thesis be handled most effectively?

Consequently, this handbook focuses not just on the honors thesis itself but on the whole range of activities that honors programs have developed to assist and improve honors thesis work. In this handbook we use the term *honors thesis program* to refer to the totality of thesis-related coursework and activities that may begin as early as the freshman year and continue even beyond the completion of the written thesis. Most commonly, an honors thesis program consists of a junior-year thesis preparation course and a senior-level *thesis course*, that is, the honors course under which the thesis is registered and graded. In addition, the wealth of materials, guidelines, advice, and tips that honors programs and colleges publish as handouts and online are clearly an important part of their honors thesis programs, as are the decision to require a formal thesis proposal, the selection of a thesis advisor in the junior year, group meetings of faculty thesis advisors, and support activities for thesis students at all stages of their work. Use of the term *thesis program* recognizes the high degree of variability in the way the honors thesis is structured in different honors programs and colleges.

In addition to such crucial activities for upper-division students and their faculty advisors, some honors thesis programs consciously highlight the honors thesis early on in an undergraduate's academic career: explaining the importance and value of the honors thesis in recruitment activities and student orientations, requiring research projects or other thesis-associated activities in lower-division honors courses, and including discussions of relevant honors theses in other honors courses by bringing senior honors students into lower-division courses to present and discuss their thesis work. At the end of their academic careers, even after the thesis has been written, students may be required to submit some reflective comments on their thesis work, its relationship to previous courses, and an analysis of their intellectual growth. At some institutions, a student's thesis work is considered completed only after the thesis has been publicly presented or defended. All of these activities can be important aspects of an honors thesis program that is committed to fostering student success and making the most of the thesis experience.

Much of the material in this handbook will already be familiar to many honors directors and deans, especially if they have a workable thesis program. But even stable and successful thesis programs often have some glitches or need some fine-tuning. We encourage the administrators of these programs to skim the material in this handbook to find support for current practices and even a new idea or two. Certainly administrators who have attended an NCHC conference or a regional honors conference have already picked up a number of ideas for improving the thesis process from presentations and informal discussions with colleagues. For administrators who are new to honors or rethinking their entire thesis program, this handbook will offer a rich and thorough compendium of common practices, options, and strategies.

In this handbook readers will find no NCHC "requirements," no absolutes, no must-dos. We offer possibilities and choices, options and practices that may prove valuable, not prescriptions or requirements. This compendium of options includes discussion of their advantages and disadvantages, which we hope honors administrators and faculty will find useful in the conceptualization of the thesis itself and its academic management, whether for a 1–3-credit thesis project at a two-year college or a multi-year 6–12-credit research-based thesis at a large university. We recognize that one size does not fit all, that some of the practices we discuss would be too costly in time and resources for smaller institutions and that others would be too unwieldy at larger ones. Still, we believe that all the ideas presented here can give every reader some food for thought and perhaps be adapted to fit the needs of individual honors programs.

A NOTE ABOUT TERMINOLOGY, CONSTRUCTION, AND CITATIONS

For the sake of clarity, brevity, and effective communication, we have tried to avoid cumbersome expressions whenever possible in this handbook. We use the term *honors thesis* to refer to the variety of culminating honors projects offered in many honors programs under the designation of "thesis," "senior project," "capstone experience," or analogous terms. We use the term *honors program* to include the whole range of honors experience at two-year schools, four-year colleges, and research institutions. We use the terms *honors director, dean,* and *administrator* to indicate all the people who have the responsibility for administering their institution's honors program or college. We use the term *thesis administrator* to include other honors program and honors college staff who have administrative responsibility for the thesis. And again, we use the term *thesis course* to refer to the final institutional structure for registering the thesis and assigning it a grade. (For further discussion of the distinction between honors programs and honors colleges, readers may find it useful to consult the NCHC monograph edited by Peter C. Sederberg, *The Honors College Phenomenon* (2008), which includes the basic characteristics of an honors program as well as the basic characteristics of an honors college. Both the monograph and the basic characteristics are available on the NCHC website: <http://www.nchchonors.org>.)

Before we began writing this handbook, we twice sent out an electronic survey to all NCHC members. The response each time was less than 10%, which made any results invalid on their own. Consequently, we talked with scores of honors deans and directors about their thesis programs, including requirements, preparation, advisement, credits, and timetables. In addition, we have led or participated in dozens of Beginning in Honors and Developing in Honors sessions at regional and national honors conferences, and we have served as consultants for numerous honors programs. All of these professional activities inform the information and assertions in this handbook.

This handbook also includes occasional comments from students, faculty, directors, and deans. These comments are taken from thesis handouts, honors handbooks, institutional websites, and personal communications to the authors of this monograph. We hope these diverse comments will underscore and enliven points we think are important and showcase a variety of approaches and responses to the thesis process. We see these comments as a collection of verbal snapshots—what students might call a mash-up—not requiring the elaborate apparatus of formal citation. Therefore, in almost all cases and at the request of the sources, we have simply included an institutional reference.

In addition, in this handbook we have consciously included more repetition of major points and ideas than would be found in a typical NCHC monograph. Honors deans, directors, and staff bring different levels of knowledge and experience about the philosophy, design, and options available for thesis work. We encourage readers to be selective or even idiosyncratic about the sections they explore. In fact, we imagine that people will most often read this handbook in sections or dip into it rather than read it at one sitting. We expect that readers will skim some material and focus more on less familiar subjects or on topics that may be of more pressing concern. We hope that some repetition of major points will make this process more effective.

Finally, we recognize and celebrate the long history NCHC members have of sharing information and assisting each other in their common pursuits. We encourage all readers of this handbook to consult their honors colleagues and honors websites at other institutions for further, more up-to-date information. The NCHC website listing of member institutions also provides easy access to telephone numbers and email contacts: <http://www.nchchonors. org/members-area/member-institutions-4/t>.

THE HONORS THESIS

A Handbook for Honors Directors, Deans, and Faculty Advisors

The scariest moment is always just before you start.

—Stephen King, *On Writing: A Memoir of the Craft*

CHAPTER 1

What Is the Value of an Honors Thesis?

W e cannot overstate the value of the honors thesis. Almost every honors program and college offers an honors thesis option, although it may be under a different label. Honors directors and deans and faculty clearly believe that their junior and senior students are prepared for and can benefit from engaging in advanced independent projects under the supervision of one or more faculty advisors. An honors thesis allows students to explore material that interests them in greater depth than is possible in a conventional course. It helps them develop their intellectual abilities and research or creative skills. It provides them with the opportunity to experience a supportive mentoring relationship with individual faculty members in their chosen area of interest. Thus, the thesis serves as the culmination of their college study and sometimes their first exposure to the professional expectations they are likely to encounter outside the academy. Numerous honors websites attest to the value of the honors thesis:

> The senior thesis is a venerable tradition in honors education in American colleges and universities. The senior thesis is promoted as the culminating product of a student's

undergraduate years, designed to showcase mastery of content, theory and methodology specific to his or her academic discipline. The term "capstone" is typically invoked to characterize the senior thesis endeavor. It is a revealing metaphor, because the capstone is that architectural component that not only ties an edifice together, but completes it: thus the senior thesis is to a large extent construed, if only subconsciously, as the final element in a student's undergraduate education. (University of Texas at Arlington)

The crowning achievement in the Honors Program is the composition of a Senior Honors Thesis or Project. (Georgetown College)

Moreover, the value of advanced undergraduate research and the thesis is endorsed throughout the academic world. Writing on the benefits of advanced undergraduate research in 2006, Tim Elgren, past president of the Council on Undergraduate Research, and Nancy Hensel, executive officer of the Council on Undergraduate Research, noted:

For good reason, undergraduate student-faculty collaborative research opportunities are firmly embedded in the landscape of the New Academy. Undergraduate research and creative expression are now distinct categories of excellence in the *U.S. News & World Report* rankings. Collaborative research speaks to some of our most fundamental educational objectives by providing a personalized education, exemplifying engaged pedagogy, and promoting students' intellectual independence and maturation. (4)

BENEFITS FOR STUDENTS

Just as honors college or program courses provide students with more challenging work in general education areas, the honors thesis offers a comparable challenge in the student's major or other area of special interest. Beyond that, the honors thesis may encourage interdisciplinary work and provide a bridge between academic study and work in the field. Furthermore, the undergraduate honors thesis is a unique opportunity for student learning, intellectual development, and even personal growth in ways not often facilitated in a conventional academic curriculum. These intellectual, personal, and practical advantages of the honors thesis are highlighted in the publications and on the websites of hundreds of honors programs or colleges.

> It broadens your horizons, and leads you to develop a sense of independence as a self-starting, highly motivated individual who can handle the challenge of a non-structured academic task. It develops organizational and "people" skills. . . . To complete this independent study project and receive a good grade, you must set the schedule, take the initiative, and discover resources in yourself that seldom come into play at the undergraduate level. You must also work closely with an advisor and build a positive relationship that will lead to successful cooperation. (University of Michigan–Flint)

> By completing an Honors Thesis, you will develop knowledge, skills and initiative that are essential to meet future challenges. You will develop self-knowledge and new personal resources. When you are pushed to the limit of your energy and creativity, you will discover new ways of addressing problems and organizing time. This training is invaluable and you will often look back to realize just how much difference it made in your professional preparation. (Clarkson University)

> When we received our first assignment [in law school], a research memo, I began immediately, because, even though an English [honors] thesis is completely different from a law school brief, I wasn't afraid of the process. The dead ends didn't scare me, didn't even frustrate me—I just plowed on. The evening before the brief was due, I was polishing while others were in the law library in tears because they'd barely

begun. I received the second highest grade in the class—the highest grade went to a paralegal who'd been doing this for several years. I couldn't have been better prepared for law school. (University of Nebraska–Lincoln)

For most students, thesis work is the natural culmination of their undergraduate careers. But for some students, the unique experience of thesis work allows them to blossom fully, sometimes in spectacular fashion, in the independent research and writing for their thesis. Every instructor has taught students with superior abilities who were somewhat reluctant participants in conventional classroom situations, students who remain withdrawn even in small seminars or very small groups. A thesis may be an eye-opening experience for some of these students, allowing them to work one-on-one with an understanding, supportive faculty member and to show what they can do on their own. The results sometimes surprise even the students themselves.

Furthermore, as honors deans and directors know, thinking about graduate or professional school needs to start well before the application process, yet sometimes even the best students cannot imagine themselves taking these paths. Thesis work and discussions with a thesis advisor may provide new insights about graduate study, financial support, and other related matters. Thesis work can hammer home to the students themselves that they have the ability to do advanced or graduate-level research. Finally, thesis work can strengthen applications to graduate or professional schools because thesis advisors are in a unique position to write detailed, meaningful letters of recommendation about the student's abilities, work ethic, and personal qualities. A letter from a professor who has worked closely with the student over an extended period of time is likely to have more weight with graduate or professional school admissions committees than a letter based on conventional classroom performance.

Let us state emphatically that honors students often do not recognize the benefits we just outlined. Some students are intimidated by the effort, originality, and commitment they believe is required to complete a thesis. Other students may want a break from college stresses in their senior year more than they want another academic challenge. In almost every college or program we have examined, honors administrators believe that too many of their students decide not to do a thesis and even drop out of the honors college or program as a consequence. Just as entering freshmen sometimes need encouragement to join an honors college or program, wavering juniors and seniors often need encouragement to undertake the thesis and reassurance that they have the ability to do well and that their efforts will be worthwhile.

Moreover, it is a rare student who does not experience feelings of confusion, helplessness, and frustration during thesis work.

> I had a rocky, love-hate relationship with my thesis paper, but it was all completely worth it. (University of Washington)

> Students who have completed a thesis often describe it as the most exciting, fulfilling, and rewarding experience of their undergraduate career, truly the capstone. At times they might use the terms frustrating, scary, and daunting. (University of Maine)

Honors directors, deans, and thesis advisors should not hesitate to discuss their own struggles as undergraduates or graduate students and to dig beneath the surface a bit with students frustrated by their own imperfections. Having a faculty member open up to students on a personal level can reassure struggling students that they are not fakes or failures, and such personal honesty often creates indelible moments in a student's undergraduate experience.

Some honors thesis programs have developed additional ways of supporting their thesis students and addressing the problems that frequently arise. Students often find meaningful support through group meetings with other thesis students who have already negotiated this unsettling academic landscape, felt the emotional swings, and survived. In colleges and programs where students are at different stages of their thesis work, peer mentoring by more advanced students can be effective. Students are often more comfortable sharing their experiences with other students than they are admitting their problems to their faculty advisors. And the more advanced students will happily share not only their difficulties but also their tips for success on a wide range of matters from dealing with faculty advisors and designing effective work plans to managing thesis projects that are stalled or expanding out of control.

Finally, social media have great potential for connecting and supporting thesis students. Because most college students check into social media daily, a thesis program might encourage student discussions on specially created websites. A listserv, a discussion space created using course management programs such as Angel or Blackboard, or even a special Facebook page can also effectively connect students. With support of this type, students struggling to complete a thesis can connect with others in a similar situation, realize that they are not the only ones scared or stalled, and profit from the coping strategies that others may discuss.

Despite the challenges, many students do see the personal and professional value of thesis work. At the end of every academic year, many honors directors encounter a student who says, "I didn't want to do it, I didn't think I could do it, but I stuck with it. And you know what? I did it. Now I know I can do whatever gets thrown at me. Thank you for pushing me beyond what I thought I could do." In addition, students who go on to graduate schools regularly report back to their undergraduate honors directors or faculty mentors about how much better prepared they are for graduate work than their non-honors classmates. Moreover, as we noted above, a thesis provides tangible evidence to graduate schools and potential employers of the student's skills and abilities. It says, "Here's what I've done!" not merely, "Here's what my undergraduate grades and test scores indicate I might be able to do." Many an honors thesis has opened doors to graduate work and employment.

> What do you talk about with a prospective employer or a medical school admission officer? What do you write about on your graduate school application? For many Honors Program students, it is their senior research or creative project. (University of Wyoming)

Clearly then, the honors thesis prepares students for graduate and professional education. While the honors thesis can often be intimidating and frustrating, perhaps the combination of both problems and triumphs makes the thesis so uniquely rewarding and such great preparation for the travails of graduate school. Thesis students have learned research skills, have mastered time management, have learned to work with faculty, and have learned to write well. Their thesis gives them an understanding of graduate-level expectations, the nature of independent work, a good introduction to professional perspectives and research methodologies, and the skills they will need to thrive. In other words, the experience provides them with a distinct advantage over non-honors students. Because of their work with their thesis advisor, they are familiar with the relationship between student and faculty that exists in graduate school, and they will have the confidence needed to complete their graduate work.

BENEFITS FOR FACULTY

Honors thesis work also has clear benefits for faculty. It demonstrates to their departments and to the institution their commitment to their students and to advanced-level education. It documents their willingness to advise and mentor students, an aspect of faculty life that too often goes unnoticed and unrecognized. Moreover, an honors thesis provides faculty members with an opportunity to collaborate with advanced students, often their best and most enthusiastic students, in an area of mutual interest. This experience can be especially valuable in an undergraduate institution where faculty do not have the opportunity to work with graduate students. The collaboration between faculty and honors students can sometimes result in jointly authored publishable papers or presentations at professional meetings. In "The Benefits of Undergraduate Research, Scholarship, and Creative Activity," Jeffrey Osborn and Kerry Karukstis explore faculty motivation for involvement in undergraduate research, such as a commitment to mentoring the promising student, maintaining the connection between teaching and research, and fostering intellectual renewal. Faculty also indicate that an important motivator is the personal satisfaction they get from working with creative and thoughtful undergrads (41–53).

The honors thesis requirement or option gives faculty a well-timed opportunity to assist their talented students in selecting and applying to graduate schools. Thesis advisors can call upon their national network of professional connections on the student's behalf, help students choose the right graduate or professional program, advise them on securing financial assistance, and connect them with colleagues who can continue the mentoring process.

> This work will make you more competitive for grants, fellowships, graduate school, or employment. In your future, you are likely to be competing for a choice job, admission to top graduate schools, or limited fellowship funding. You need to do more to distinguish yourself than just get good grades in your courses and score well on exams such as the GRE, MCAT, or LSAT. You can gain an edge on the competition if you plan your project early, do impressive work, and end your undergraduate career with a tangible accomplishment that your letter of reference writers can talk about in detail. Find something you can get excited about working on, and use your imagination in developing your plan. The sky is the limit! (Grand Valley State University)

Most faculty members report that they derive great professional and personal satisfaction from their work mentoring an honors thesis—the satisfaction of helping a student reach his or her intellectual potential, the satisfaction of working with the best and the brightest students on campus, and of course the many pleasures of new research projects and discoveries. Faculty also recognize that thesis work takes time away from their other commitments and sometimes presents them with real frustrations. But in the end most would strongly endorse the following statement: "This honors student is the type of student I always hoped to teach and mentor. My experience as an honors thesis advisor reminds me of the reasons why I chose to become a college teacher."

BENEFITS FOR THE HONORS PROGRAM OR HONORS COLLEGE AND THE UNIVERSITY

Honors thesis work has benefits beyond those for individual students and faculty. In particular, thesis work offers significant benefits for the honors program or college and for the institution as a whole. By its very nature the thesis provides the honors program or college and its students with a desirable visibility on campus. Increased visibility helps to justify increased institutional support. It lays the groundwork for additional faculty participation in the honors program or college's courses and activities, widening the pool of professors who may want to teach honors courses in the future. Sadly, even tenured faculty members sometimes are unaware of or have forgotten about the honors program until a student approaches them with a request to work with them on a thesis. When some of the best students in a department discuss their theses with faculty, both faculty and departments feel that they have an active stake in the success of the honors program.

Moreover, an honors thesis program can bring diverse faculty from across campus together for meetings of thesis advisors, colloquia, or online discussions, providing faculty who might otherwise have little contact outside their own area with opportunities for interaction and discussion. Sometimes these contacts can generate new ideas for research, joint projects, or even the development of new interdisciplinary or multidisciplinary courses. In other words, just as an honors program provides students with an opportunity for enriched study, so thesis work can offer faculty an occasion for intellectual stimulation and interchange. An undergraduate thesis program fosters, as Osborn and Karukstits observe, "a self-perpetuating social infrastructure," bringing faculty together for "innovation and cross-talk" and a shared sense of purpose (46–47).

For both an honors program or college and the institution as a whole, the honors thesis embodies the highest level of undergraduate work. In an honors curriculum, the thesis elevates and focuses the intellectual challenges of honors work into a culminating project that can be extremely attractive, albeit intimidating, to students.

For this reason, honors programs and colleges often include in their publications some profiles of senior honors students and their thesis work. The impact of these narratives about independent research or the personal relationship with their faculty mentors as well as student testimonials about the value of this experience should not be underestimated. For some entering freshmen, the opportunity to do independent research with a mentoring faculty member may be a significant factor in their decision to enroll at a particular institution. Just as importantly, because thesis work offers a clear path for advanced work in an area of major interest, it may help to retain some of the outstanding students who might otherwise be tempted to transfer to another college or university for their last two years.

Some institutions seem almost as proud of their honors theses as they are of their athletic successes. College or university publications often include stories of student research and summarize recently completed thesis projects. Community relations officers recognize that profiles of senior honors students make great copy and that honors theses are clear examples of academic excellence to the outside world. In an age when attention is strongly focused on learning outcomes and the evaluation of faculty and programs, the honors thesis highlights the importance of honors activities for the college or university and provides substantive evidence of student success, educational progress, and high-level achievement, evidence that honors deans and directors can document easily and that upper-level administrators can understand and use to their advantage. Many institutions embrace a measurement model that considers the number of student theses that are completed in a department or at the institution as a whole to be important indicators of academic excellence. As Osborn and Karukstis note, the benefits of undergraduate research projects can extend even to the "national recognition received when results of student and faculty work are disseminated and the receipt of external funding when grant proposals are successful" (46).

Finally, an honors thesis program can benefit the institution by expanding connections to alumni, potential donors, and the greater community. In the course of their thesis work, honors students sometimes connect with relevant alumni, community leaders, or specialists in their field. This contact is likely to create a positive impression on behalf of the institution. Some honors programs and colleges actively encourage alumni to sponsor the research expenses of thesis students, thereby further strengthening alumni connection, commitment, and financial support to the institution. Alumni can easily see the value of contributing a few hundred dollars to support a thesis in the area of their former major, and rather than reducing other financial support for the institution, such personal contributions often foster increased giving in other areas.

CHAPTER 2

The Concept of the Honors Thesis

A BRIEF HISTORY OF THE HONORS THESIS

The concept of the honors thesis cuts across the practices of individual disciplines and transcends regional and national differences, in part because the concept of the honors thesis is directly connected to the earliest stages of university education in Europe and its evolution since then throughout the world. The medieval *disputatio*—a discussion and debate of texts, issues, or intellectual propositions, i.e., "theses"—was frequently the concluding element for a series of university lectures. Medieval universities embraced this public demonstration of mastery as an appropriate means of testing a student's knowledge and skills.

By the Reformation, the *disputatio* had begun its evolution beyond a demonstration of dialectal skills and articulation of received ideas. Increasingly, it functioned as an exploration of genuine problems, a type of intellectual inquiry often focused on defending truths against counterarguments. Not long afterward, it was adapted into a written form, first as a summary of the oral

15

disputatio and then as the preferred form for printed treatises, especially when they focused on innovative ideas, controversial topics, or the results of personal research. Today, the various practices now seen as the concluding element of university education at the bachelor's, master's, and doctoral levels—thesis, dissertation, and oral defense—derive from the *disputatio*, the capstone element in the early university. And even more importantly, the academic world still shares the conviction that a thesis requirement is appropriate for superior students concluding programs of advanced study.

During the late nineteenth and early twentieth centuries, a strong reform movement developed in American higher education. Some educators were concerned that the standardized curriculum at American colleges and universities was fostering mediocrity rather than excellence. Student learning, they believed, would be much improved by enriching the coursework in a student's major and minor disciplines, especially through more individualized instruction, small seminars, in-depth elective study, and a focus on student research. (For more, see Haskins, *The Rise of Universities*, and Guzy, *Honors Composition: Historical Perspectives and Contemporary Practices*.)

Both the development of honors programs and the introduction of the honors thesis for superior undergraduate students resulted from these reform efforts. A few institutions implemented comprehensive curricular reforms to foster such enrichment. Most notably, in 1922, Frank Aydelotte, who had been one of the first Rhodes Scholars and had been impressed with the Oxford approach to education, introduced a number of small, elective departmental seminars for superior students at Swarthmore College, replacing the standard required courses in the participating departments. Although other elements of honors work at Swarthmore, such as the substitution of comprehensive senior exams for seminar grades and an extensive reliance on external examiners, have been difficult for most institutions to follow, Aydelotte's conception of small honors seminars emphasizing in-depth study, interactive discussions, and close faculty-student relationships became the model for honors seminars across the country.

The majority of American colleges and universities attempting to implement honors education, however, focused on the undergraduate thesis. Starting in 1883, the University of Michigan gave honors recognition at graduation to students who had completed an undergraduate thesis and an approved selection of courses. By the 1920s, honors enrichment was taking place in undergraduate curricula nationwide, and an honors thesis course was adopted at one institution after another as a means to this end. When the National Research Council surveyed honors options for superior students at the member institutions of the Association of American Colleges and Universities, Aydellote was asked to edit the results of the survey. His report, published in 1924 in the *Bulletin of the National Research Council,* showed that while 9 institutions had attempted to create an alternative curriculum for honors students as Swarthmore had done, many more—80% of the institutions (36 out of 45)—had added the honors thesis as their primary focus of enrichment. When Aydellote completed a similar survey the next year, the numbers had roughly doubled in all areas, but the ratios remained the same, with about 75 institutions requiring an undergraduate thesis for honors graduation.

Almost a century after Aydellote's surveys, honors enrichment is firmly established in the majority of American colleges and universities, in many two-year and technical colleges, and in many institutions of higher learning throughout the world. Clearly, the conception of student-as-junior-researcher, inherent in the model of the nineteenth-century German research university and especially fostered by the educational principles associated with Wilhelm von Humboldt, principally the unity of teaching and research and the importance of student freedom in choosing subjects to be studied, continues to be of widespread importance in the honors community (Albritton 2006). The honors thesis is the clearest embodiment of this educational paradigm, offering learning through research, incorporating close faculty mentoring, and honoring the independent work and original insights of student researchers.

Unfortunately, at the same time many pressures are working against the traditional, liberal-arts-based honors thesis and expensive faculty mentoring of individual student researchers. The pressures for mass education, the use of adjuncts and support staff as replacements for full-time faculty, the increasing professional (rather than research) focus in some areas of disciplinary work, and the movement towards online learning have often reduced the personal contact between tenure-track faculty members and students. Moreover, students' undergraduate careers are increasingly disjointed; spread over multiple institutions, commonly incorporating internships and foreign study experiences; and sometimes interrupted by childrearing, work, or a change in career interests. Consequently, many institutions struggle to incorporate a solid honors thesis into this new learning environment, even for a limited number of superior students.

Yet, the undergraduate thesis, in general, and the honors thesis, in particular, still retain many advantages in this context. Undergraduate thesis requirements ensure that a productive and personal faculty-student mentorship is a significant part of students' advanced studies in their disciplines, especially when many of their other studies have been in large classes or online. Moreover, it is not inconceivable that the honors thesis may emerge both as a valued integrative experience for the diverse elements of students' academic careers, as an interactive experience in which students become research partners with their faculty mentors, and as a capstone course that enables the graduating institution to assess (and perhaps certify) total student learning and the level of student achievement.

DEPARTMENTAL CONTROL OF THE HONORS THESIS

The traditional honors thesis was based on the assumption that students would find a research project in their major and work under the supervision of a faculty member in that department. Since college work in the United States typically moves from general education courses to specialized requirements and electives in a major field, thesis work in a student's final year fits this academic trajectory. In their last two years of study, undergraduates are highly focused on courses, topics, and research projects in their major; this major is often connected to students' expectations for their adult life and work after graduation. Moreover, thesis work on a specialized project in their major field is essentially a further manifestation of disciplinary specialization. Often the topics that students select for their honors theses are those that engaged them in one of their upper-division courses, and the faculty member who taught this course emerges as the logical choice to be the thesis advisor.

This departmental orientation of the thesis usually functions well: students have a clear understanding of the disciplinary approaches and assumptions in their major field, they have completed specialized coursework in their specific area of research and related areas, and the faculty advisor's knowledge of the student's abilities and the student's knowledge of the faculty member's expectations provide a promising start for a sound mentoring relationship. Moreover, these activities generate few costs and some obvious benefits. As a part of their departmental responsibilities, individual faculty members can teach their thesis students on a tutorial basis outside of normal course scheduling, other departmental support is readily available, and the awarding of an honors designation for the thesis provides a departmental imprimatur for the student's achievement.

Consequently, from its beginnings, honors thesis work fit easily under the control of the individual departments that offered this option. The thesis option and/or program of honors study could be limited to those students departmental faculty believed were qualified for independent research projects in their discipline. The departments conferred honors distinctions at graduation. Students graduated with honors in Art History or Chemistry or English, often decades before institutional honors programs developed at their colleges or universities. When college- or university-wide honors programs developed in the twentieth century, they almost always began by embracing the scattered islands of departmental honors and thesis programs on their campus, often allowing them to continue as relatively autonomous departmental programs.

Most institutions accepted the model of the department-based honors thesis as their standard practice. Departmental faculty traditionally had and continue to have the responsibility for defining the scope and nature of an honors thesis, as well as for determining the number of credits to be assigned for an individual thesis project. And without question, the departmental faculty still accept primary responsibility for the students doing an honors thesis in their disciplines. They direct student research, advise students when difficulties arise, evaluate the quality of the thesis (even whether or not it qualifies for "honors"), and assign it a grade. Departmental honors programs sometimes operate with almost complete autonomy, selecting and recruiting their outstanding majors for honors thesis work, whether they have taken any other honors coursework or not. Conversely, a departmental program may decide that a successful student in the institution's honors program or college is not qualified for the departmental honors thesis program.

Today, departmental expectations and control continue to be major factors in defining honors thesis work. Although some honors thesis courses may be registered through a college or university honors program, most thesis courses are registered as departmental courses, following historical precedent and student preferences for thesis projects in their major. Departmental programs may also specifically define the preparation that students need for thesis work in their discipline. Because departmental faculty understand the demands and potential problems of thesis projects in their areas, they sometimes require other coursework, seminars, or tutorials in conjunction with the thesis project. A department may establish specific prerequisites, such as additional research courses, previous research work, required fieldwork, language immersion, or volunteer/internship experience, for students who wish to do a thesis in their discipline.

These departmental requirements suggest that faculty strongly believe that some additional preparation for students embarking on a thesis will help them to produce higher quality theses at higher completion rates. An English department may decide to spread thesis work over two terms, with the first term consisting of a seminar devoted to the development of research plans and a rough draft of the first chapter, and the second term focused on independent research, meetings with the thesis advisor, and writing and rewriting of the thesis. A history department may have a thesis prep course focused on working with primary sources, a sociology department may require an advanced research methods course, and an art department may require a seminar on best practices for designing an art exhibition. Additionally, departments may bring their students together for research seminars, group discussions, or online interactions through classroom management programs or social media in conjunction with a thesis course to address common problems and to build a sense of community among thesis students.

THE ROLE OF THE HONORS PROGRAM IN THESIS MANAGEMENT

In recent years, honors programs and colleges have begun to provide a great deal of encouragement, support, and institutional oversight for students writing an undergraduate thesis. The very existence of an honors program or college and its thesis requirement promotes undergraduate thesis work throughout the institution as an integral part of a superior program of study. Moreover, an honors program provides the institution and its faculty with a steady stream of superior students interested in senior research projects and looking for faculty to guide them. These students, as well as their advisors, typically view their honors work, especially their thesis work, as a focal point of their academic experience, one they will highlight in their applications for graduate schools, professional schools, and employment opportunities. These students are also usually among those highlighted by departments in their annual reports. In effect, students who complete an honors thesis become examples of student excellence at the college or university. Everyone at an institution, therefore, has a vested interest in making the undergraduate honors thesis as valuable and as successful as possible.

The value of the honors program's involvement in successful thesis work cannot be overstated, even at those institutions where strong and autonomous departments control the thesis. During the last few decades, many institutions have moved beyond simply requiring a thesis and have created what we would call an *honors thesis program*: a framework of courses, faculty mentoring, and institutional support that focuses both on students preparing to begin the thesis and those already in the thick of it, rather than just handing off upper-division students to their thesis advisors and major departments.

A comprehensive honors thesis program typically introduces students to the idea of the honors thesis in their lower-division honors courses, presenting it as a natural development in the academic career of students and then providing a smooth transition into actual thesis work in their last two years of college. Assignments in lower-division honors courses can introduce students to the rhetorical and research skills that they will need to complete a thesis. A thesis program can provide students with extensive information in printed handbooks, online materials, or a series of specialized handouts related to thesis work and covering more than just the basic thesis requirements. A thesis program can help students understand how to select a thesis topic or a thesis advisor, how to approach time management, and how to make the most of meetings with their thesis advisor. Finally, at many colleges and universities the central part of the honors thesis program is a thesis preparation course that jumpstarts the thesis process. (For a further discussion of the thesis prep course, see Chapter 4.)

A particularly important part of an honors thesis program is its ability to provide students with ongoing advisement and support. While most departmental honors programs can focus only on their upper-division students, an honors thesis program can introduce students at all levels in the honors program or college to thesis work and its rewards. An honors program or college is especially well suited to provide layer upon layer of guidance and assistance for students throughout their undergraduate careers. For students who are not sure about the value of the thesis or how it could fit with their other plans, honors advisement can be an effective catalyst for realizing that thesis work is a desirable and achievable part of an undergraduate career. Honors advisement can move students from mixed feelings, indecisiveness, and procrastination into early contact with potential thesis advisors.

Honors deans, directors, and staff have experience dealing with the complex goals, aspirations, and needs of superior students, and they are especially attuned to the fact that honors students are often eager to pursue a variety of options in their undergraduate careers, including multiple majors and minors. Although these students may have little difficulty mastering a discipline, they often struggle to decide among their many interests and diverse academic options, a struggle that intensifies as their undergraduate careers advance. They often face personal and professional choices that have no easy resolutions: honors thesis research vs. foreign study, a second major and/or minor, internships, campus leadership roles, or even athletics and volunteer work. Honors administrators and staff can help students see the bigger picture and find possible paths to accommodate both the thesis and some, if not all, of their other opportunities. When an honors program provides its thesis students and their advisors with early and ongoing support that is attuned to those students trying to juggle thesis work with other activities, thesis quality and completion rates are likely to improve.

Other parts of an honors thesis program can provide valuable support to faculty in their work with thesis students. This support is particularly important at smaller institutions or at colleges and universities where departmental honors programs are not a strong presence. An honors thesis program can easily coordinate thesis work throughout an institution by establishing common deadlines for thesis completion and the required format for its submission. It can create standard forms for such tasks as thesis registration and approval, as well as providing graduation checkout for honors designations and archiving completed theses for the institution. Such activities significantly remove some of the routine work and other burdens from faculty advisors, making their contacts with students more productive and ensuring that the institution has clear and consistent expectations for thesis work. An honors thesis program certifies the completed thesis not just as superior work in a department but also as a valued *institutional* accomplishment carrying the institution's imprimatur. Finally, the honors thesis program can often provide public recognition during honors graduation ceremonies of the valuable contributions made by faculty thesis advisors. And, of course, an honors director or dean is always a valuable resource who can provide outside testimony to a department or dean about the quality of an individual thesis advisor's work.

An honors program or college is also in a unique position to offer direct assistance to faculty advisors. The only experience with thesis advisement that many faculty members have had, especially newer faculty, is whatever they encountered in their own master's or doctoral work. They may have little or no experience advising undergraduate research and even less knowledge of the requirements for undergraduate honors theses. Only in rare cases do faculty receive systematic guidance about honors thesis work from their departments, and some faculty are hesitant to ask a more experienced colleague about honors theses for fear of looking incompetent.

Unless honors programs provide some effective assistance for new thesis advisors, as well as clear written guidelines for thesis work, honors directors and deans may be faced with many problems that could have been prevented or with a great many honors theses that are highly inconsistent in quality. Hence, many honors programs not only produce extensive guidelines for thesis work for their students but also make sure that such materials get into the hands of faculty advisors. Some honors programs and colleges publish special handbooks for faculty advisors, including guidelines, expectations, timelines, best practices for mentoring, and how to deal with common problems in thesis work. All of these materials will be most effective if they are both printed and available online. In addition, successful honors programs also bring faculty advisors together in special gatherings where veteran advisors share their insights and experiences in thesis advising. Alternatively, an honors program or college can establish a system whereby experienced faculty advisors mentor faculty who are new to undergraduate thesis work.

Above all, the strong and continuing involvement of the honors program in the process of thesis work can ensure that high standards are maintained throughout the institution for the honors thesis. Such efforts may even help an institution clarify inconsistencies in course offerings. For example, at some institutions course numbers and descriptions do not distinguish honors thesis work from research courses, independent study courses, and non-honors theses. An honors program or college can be the catalyst for the institution to be consistent in its course numbering, perhaps with the honors thesis courses in every department designated with the same number, such as XXX 499; English 499: Honors Thesis; Chemistry 499: Honors Research; or Psychology 499: Honors Thesis Project.

THE TRADITIONAL HONORS THESIS:
A CAPSTONE PROJECT

In the not-too-distant past, thesis work came at the end of a hierarchical program of study, from general education to specialized courses in a discipline; from advanced courses to independent research; from smaller research papers to a larger, deeper, and culminating thesis research project. Student development and academic careers were carefully controlled, with the honors thesis occupying the last stage, the capstone level. In contrast to earlier coursework, the honors thesis at this level was meant to give more scope to the student's originality and independent work.

In this context "originality" for the honors project meant study beyond standard course content, assignments, and papers. It meant that students designed their own research projects rather than having them assigned, and it highlighted the student's own insights and conclusions rather than the received ideas that often dominated traditional coursework. "Independent" research meant no required class texts, no fixed assigned course meetings, and no intrusive examinations. The specific thesis project determined the appropriate readings, students and advisors agreed on convenient meeting times, and the thesis itself determined the student's grade. Still, students engaged in independent research were not permitted to wander off on their own. Faculty thesis advisors monitored and guided the "independent" research closely, working in a tutorial/mentoring role.

Today the concepts of originality and independent research sometimes owe more to the dictates of faculty research than they do to the realities of undergraduate study. Although one often hears the terms "originality" and "original research" in discussions of honors theses, these concepts today are so weighed down by the expectations of faculty research that some faculty struggle to understand what would be realistic expectations for an undergraduate honors thesis. At the back of their minds, these faculty believe that the "original" work required for an undergraduate honors thesis should meet almost the same standard for academic activity that is expected of them: work that breaks new ground in a specific area of research, work worthy of publication. These high standards too often lead to frustrated and unsatisfactory faculty interactions with their honors thesis students.

Are such standards, however, really appropriate for undergraduates? True, one Princeton undergraduate used his research project to discover the means of constructing a viable atomic bomb. (See Phillips and Michaelis, 1978.) But similar discoveries are rare. We need to be honest here: most honors directors and deans recognize that few undergraduates, including even the brightest and most dedicated honors students, even those intending to become rocket scientists, lack the time or the training to produce an original contribution to a discipline's knowledge base. Yes, David Foster Wallace and others have turned their honors theses into successful books or substantial articles, and some honors theses are published in professional or student journals. (See Peterson, 2009.) Others win impressive national prizes such as the NCHC's Portz awards, and a great many other students present their thesis work at regional or national conferences. But most honors theses, even the outstanding ones—as well as most master's theses or doctoral dissertations—are rarely, if ever, consulted in professional research projects or listed in standard disciplinary bibliographies of significant publications.

If honors administrators focus on the important place of the honors thesis in most undergraduates' careers, more appropriate expectations for thesis work become clear. Even without a hierarchical curriculum, the honors thesis has a valuable function as a capstone to undergraduate studies, as a culminating project that draws on the student's previous study and experience. For students, the thesis does not necessarily embody their most original ideas. Rather, it allows them to demonstrate their mastery of a specific subject matter, their familiarity with the practices and conventions in a discipline, and their qualifications for future independent work. Hence, it is similar to the final projects of apprentices, which prove their mastery of a trade and qualify them for admittance as full members of a guild or union. In such work, whether by an apprentice or an honors student, the finished product may not have the mastery, quality, and polish comparable to that of an experienced professional, but it does reflect the potential for such achievement in the future.

The place of the thesis in an undergraduate's final year at a four-year institution restricts the scope of the thesis. The thesis does not need to be a huge, groundbreaking research project; a smaller project is sufficient to demonstrate a student's mastery of his or her discipline and a capacity for independent work. Hence, the honors thesis is typically tied to a single thesis course, usually a 3–4-credit course, although a preparatory course may also be required as a prerequisite to thesis work, and some honors thesis programs require a larger thesis course or extend it over a year or two. (See Chapter 4.)

When it comes to credits, as a general rule the thesis course—in which the student registers the thesis and receives a grade—should follow the institution's established policies for the relationship between work expected and credits awarded. Because thesis work must fit into an undergraduate's schedule, which normally includes other demanding courses and obligations, a student may need to adjust the scope of the thesis project to fit the time available. If this shift is not possible, the student may have to find another topic that can be completed within the time constraints.

Most institutions do not permit undergraduates to register repeatedly for a thesis course to complete their thesis work, a practice common for masters and doctoral students. There is a strong expectation that undergraduates should complete their coursework, including the thesis, by the end of their last term in college. Experienced honors deans and directors can testify that few problems are more vexing and less easily resolved than those posed by students who do not complete the honors thesis before they leave campus at the end of their undergraduate careers. Despite the flexibility that characterizes much of the contemporary world of academe, educators still expect undergraduates to make steady progress towards graduation, to complete the thesis while enrolled in other courses, and even to graduate on time with their peers. Responding to these demands is another reason why educators prize the honors thesis and admire the honors students who do it.

In most honors programs the thesis itself, rather than a particular grade, satisfies the honors thesis requirement. In some cases, therefore, allowing a student to register a thesis for fewer credits than is usually acceptable may be appropriate. Sometimes this situation occurs when a student has done work in an advanced research course or a non-honors thesis course offered by the major department. When the product of this research meets the quality standards and other requirements for an honors thesis, honors administrators can accept it without additional work and certainly without having the student register twice for the same work.

In many cases, however, work completed in a non-honors course may need beefing up to meet the honors thesis requirements: selective revisions or specific additions such as more systematic documentation of a performance project, more issue-oriented discussion and argumentation, or the addition of reflective comments on the student's academic development and thesis experience. Students are often permitted to register for 1–2 credits for this additional work to meet honors thesis standards and requirements. Finally, at some institutions a thesis student may face additional per-credit charges or may be constrained by the maximum number of credit hours allowed per term. In such cases, the student might be allowed to register for a reduced 1–2 thesis credits while completing the work that would normally be done for a 3–4-credit thesis.

Students at two-year colleges obviously do not have the longer time frame that students at a four-year institution have to plan and complete a thesis. Most two-year colleges, therefore, do not have a thesis requirement; however, some offer students the opportunity to complete what is typically referred to as an honors project. Such projects may be an outgrowth of an honors course; the further development of an assignment done for a course in the student's area of interest, perhaps with additional requirements for research and public presentation; or a one- or two-term faculty-guided independent study. Such honors projects serve many of the same functions as the honors thesis and offer an integrating and culminating honors experience for students in two-year programs.

BASIC ELEMENTS OF AN HONORS THESIS

Despite widespread agreement about the objectives of the honors thesis, the thesis is difficult to define and especially difficult to explain to students. Students usually think of an honors thesis as similar to work they have done before. They view it primarily as a glorified term paper, a big research paper, or as a larger, more demanding version of a required project they have done in the past. And, to a certain extent, this observation is true. Previous student work should indeed have prepared them for the honors thesis; many theses do require a great deal of library research; and most do place heavy emphasis on producing a written text, "the thesis." An honors thesis, however, need not be just a traditional research project or be limited to a written document. It can also be an art exhibition, a theatre or dance performance, a marketing plan, or a software program. Although traditional theses may take standard forms in some disciplines, contemporary students are also interested in new approaches that enable them to combine some of their diverse interests. Thus, an honors thesis is an elusive creature to define.

As we noted, one of the distinguishing features of the honors thesis is its function as the capstone to a student's undergraduate career; it is not simply a term paper or an independent study report. Students may pursue independent study at almost any time during their academic careers. The project may involve extended reading, even a bit of research, but not necessarily original thinking. Independent study usually involves exploring a topic or area not covered by an institution's registered courses, relying on independent learning outside the classroom context. The only requirement is that the student find a professor who supports the student's proposed "study" and is willing to give him or her a grade at the end of the semester. Such an independent study may involve little or no writing, no thesis that must be proved, and no specified meetings with or mentoring by the faculty member.

By contrast, the honors thesis is specifically intended for students nearing the end of their undergraduate careers. The honors thesis is advanced level work that focuses on *an explicit thesis:* a question to be answered, a problem to be solved, an analysis of central issues, and ultimately a position to be explained. Hence thesis students are expected to choose topics for exploration that incorporate their previous study and learning, involve some original analysis, and result in significant research or creative projects. Because of these intellectual demands, most theses require a formal proposal, including a carefully considered research plan that functions, in a sense, as a contract between student and advisor. The thesis proposal frequently must be approved not only by the thesis advisor but also by the department, the student's college, and/or the honors director or dean.

While research courses and independent study courses simply conclude with a grade given at the end of the term, an honors thesis usually has additional requirements. An honors thesis typically requires a substantial written component, even for performance-based projects; student documentation according to professional standards in the field; and a successful public presentation or defense of the thesis. An honors thesis is truly intended to be the student's culminating experience, worthy of public dissemination and exemplifying undergraduate academic achievement at its highest level.

Because of their own experience writing a graduate-level thesis or dissertation, faculty sometimes overestimate the level of scholarship an undergraduate honors student can achieve in a thesis. An honors thesis is not the equivalent of a research paper for a graduate seminar, nor is it just a short master's thesis. The scope, time requirement, and standards for such theses and dissertations far exceed those appropriate for an undergraduate honors thesis. Yet the honors thesis should be more substantial than an ordinary undergraduate term paper or a research paper from a senior seminar. The thesis project should surpass the scope and quality of research work done as a part of a typical research methods course, yet be a project that can be developed within the limitations of an undergraduate's understanding and experience. An honors thesis should represent research and in-depth knowledge of the field, even if it is not a traditional research project. Finally, it must be of a reasonable length and stay within the abilities of a student who has spent only a part of his or her undergraduate career taking courses in a major.

Thus, the definition of an honors thesis is necessarily a pragmatic one: *the honors thesis is a large research or creative project that can be pursued successfully in one-to-four semesters as part of a normal undergraduate course load.* To put it simply, an honors thesis should be superior undergraduate work that reflects high standards of quality in its ideas, methodology, accuracy, clarity, reasoning, and presentation—not simply work that might earn an A in a classroom or an Independent Study. This conception of the thesis is inescapably ambiguous because it must encompass a vast number of disciplines and a wide variety of approaches. A thesis may be a "traditional" research study, but it also may be a collaborative, creative, pre-professional, interdisciplinary project or a combination of these.

A number of factors clearly shape all thesis work: the capabilities, experience, and interests of the student producing the thesis; the discipline; the scope of the project; the time frame in which the institution or program requires the thesis to be completed; the resources available to the student; and the demands on both student and faculty member. One of the tasks for an honors director is to make sure that the faculty thesis advisors' expectations are realistic and appropriate for undergraduates and to repeatedly communicate appropriate thesis standards to thesis advisors, new and old, through handouts, handbooks for faculty advisors, and email or online materials.

Appropriate Originality and Scope

Honors directors, deans, and faculty should recognize that most undergraduates, even those in honors programs and colleges, are frequently unaware or only vaguely aware of what constitutes "original research" in a field. For most of their academic career, students have been assigned specific topics to study or have been given free range in their choice of topics, but too often little or no guidance. As a consequence, many undergraduates have only a limited understanding of "original": for many students it means little more than an extended book report or library research, with a page or two of sources contained in a bibliography—not including Wikipedia!

Hence, honors programs and thesis advisors must help students recognize that real intellectual effort is required to conceptualize, organize, and carry out a successful thesis project. In many honors thesis programs, a required early start to thesis work, typically in the junior year, presses home to students the sizable new demands of the honors thesis. By having students select their faculty advisors at this time and preparing them for the discussion, revision, and rewriting of their thesis proposal, the honors thesis program emphasizes that much more is involved in crafting a successful thesis than just the simple selection of a topic. Thus students are both presented with the challenges of thesis work and given the appropriate solutions: a sizable honors thesis can be successful if begun early, and the student's original ideas will benefit from the expertise of a faculty advisor. (See Chapter 4 for further discussion of the thesis preparation course.)

One of the first questions students ask about an honors thesis is, "How long does it have to be?" The obvious answer is that there is no standard length for an honors thesis. Although thesis work tends to be more substantial than that required in a normal course paper both in terms of effort and size, the specific length of the finished thesis depends on the area of study, the topic, and of course common practices at individual institutions. A traditional research thesis in art history, English, or sociology might be 50–60 pages—or more. Supreme Court Justice Sonya Sotomayor's Princeton undergraduate honors thesis in history, "La Historia Ciclica de Puerto Rico: The Impact of the Life of Luis Muñoz Marin on the Political and Economic History of Puerto Rico, 1930–1975," was 178 pages long! (See Winn, 2009.) In a number of fields, however, such as the sciences or performing arts, the written part of the thesis may be significantly shorter even though it requires the same effort.

Honors directors and deans can often address the question of thesis length and required work by presenting students with norms and ranges. For example, they can explain that most honors theses in history at their institution have been about 50 pages long, with 3–5 pages of primary and secondary documentation. Most art students who do an exhibition of their paintings have displayed 20 pieces or so; written a 10–20-page text that explains their objectives, influences, choices, and themes; and perhaps provided photos or a video documenting their work. A computer program, engineering application, or dance performance that forms the basis for a thesis could be clarified in similar ways.

Honors directors and thesis advisors should recognize that seemingly naïve student questions about thesis length and the required number of sources actually point to deeper concerns. Students are really trying to find out, "How much work am I going to have to do?" Just like faculty investigating a possible committee assignment, the student also has another important but unarticulated question: "Is all this effort going to be worth it to me?" Honors directors and faculty advisors need to address both of these questions if they hope to provide appropriate guidance for their students. To aid their students in understanding normal expectations for the thesis, many honors directors and thesis advisors have their current students read several similar theses completed in past years. Once students have some grasp of what a thesis entails, they almost always respond by saying, "That doesn't look so hard. I can do that!"

Problem Solving

At its heart, every good honors thesis is an exercise in problem solving. This problem solving exists in every field, from a biology student's deciding what kind of analysis to use to measure water quality, to a history student's trying to determine the reliability of a primary source, to an English student's evaluation of various scholarly arguments about Hamlet's paralysis. From the thesis proposal that defines the scope of the intellectual quest, through the research or creative methodologies that the student utilizes, to the structure of the final thesis, every step in the process involves choices. One of the most important tasks for honors administrators and for honors thesis advisors is framing the thesis experience in ways that will help students recognize the existence of critical choices in every endeavor, the importance of problem solving in their work, and the need to make these choices from an informed perspective that reflects an awareness of the views and practices of others present and past. All of these elements are encompassed in the idea of research embodied in the honors thesis.

Sometimes students completing a fine arts or performance thesis, and even some faculty advisors, believe that this problem solving is overly intellectual and does not mesh with their discipline. For example, an art student may say, "This is my vision of the world, and I want to communicate it through my painting." The same applies to students working in poetry or theatre, sculpture or dance, fiction or photography. The honors dean or director must help students understand that underlying this desire for personal and creative expression is a series of problems the student needs to solve: What is the most effective medium to communicate my vision? What form should it take? What shall I select to exhibit? What styles should I draw on—or reject? Whose earlier work has influenced me? And how?

In addition to this intellectual problem solving, every honors thesis also requires that students learn to solve the practical problems that arise in pursuit of their thesis. Students not only have to solve the intellectual problems they encounter in their field of study or creative endeavor, but they also must learn to navigate deadlines, deal with their advisors' desires and often different viewpoints, and comply with college regulations. In fact, we find that, after students have completed their thesis, what they remember most vividly is not always the content or the details of what they did; what they find most important are the problem-solving skills they developed along the way, the satisfaction of having made effective choices, and the feeling of accomplishment that comes from the impact these choices had on the direction and quality of their thesis. As veteran honors administrators know, students most often fail to complete the thesis not because of intellectual deficiency but rather because of poor project strategies, such as a failure to schedule regular meetings with their thesis advisor, an inability to structure their work to meet deadlines, and the inevitable procrastination that seems endemic within an academic setting. Thus, the mastery we spoke about above is not merely of the subject matter; it is also a mastery of the process.

Written Work

Almost every honors program or college requires that an honors thesis have a written component. Whether the thesis has at its core traditional research in the sciences, the humanities, or the social sciences or features a creative project, an exhibition, or a performance, students are expected to produce some written work that describes, analyzes, and documents their research or project. In the humanities, research is typically presented as a written text that analyzes primary documents and the viewpoints of others as it argues its thesis. In the social sciences, the written text and analysis of issues remain central, although greater emphasis may be placed on data analysis. In the sciences, while the answer to the research question is always significant, the heart of the research lies in the proof or explanation of how the answer was reached.

Theses in drama, art, music, or creative writing may appropriately emphasize the creative act, non-verbal materials, or a performance as a central element of the thesis. An art student might create an exhibition of original works, a theater major might direct a play, or a creative writing major might compose a collection of short stories. In most honors programs and colleges, however, while such a project can form the *basis* of a thesis, it is not considered to be a thesis in and of itself.

Most honors programs and colleges require the author of a creative thesis to supplement the work by a written description, analysis, or evaluation. This portion of the work might include, but not be limited to, a discussion of the exhibition, performance, story, or script. This piece might address such questions as who or what sparked the student's creative vision for the project, why the student took that particular approach, why he or she* selected the particular work or works to be performed, or what the student might do differently (or the same) next time. Honors thesis administrators might find it useful to think of the written description and analysis as material that frames and contextualizes the creative work. In addition to the written component, final submission of a creative thesis often includes an appropriate record of the project, such as photographs, working sketches and layouts, a portfolio, and audio or video files.

The pragmatic thesis is another type of thesis: it typically offers an action plan for or a solution to an existing problem. Examples of this type of thesis might include the creation of a computer program or an Internet website; the preparation of a public awareness campaign, branding strategy, or marketing plan; the study of community needs and resources for a non-profit organization; the design and pilot implementation of educational curricula and classroom materials; or a sports training program. Again, like the creative thesis, the pragmatic thesis should include a written analysis that contextualizes the project and includes appropriate documentation.

*See Russo, 1997.

Self-Reflection

Some honors programs and colleges also require a self-reflective component as part of the honors thesis, believing that it has great value. This reflective section can be a preface to the body of the thesis or an appendix, usually no longer than 3-to-5 pages. While this part of a thesis may seem to be a recent invention, it actually has roots in the comments scholars and scribes added to the margins and colophons of their manuscripts. Their personal comments often focus on their writing and its difficulties in ways that resonate strongly with contemporary students. Michael Camille's *Image on the Edge: The Margins of Medieval Art* (2013) collects a number of these early personal reflections:

- "Thank god, it will soon be dark."
- "Now I've written the whole thing: for Christ's sake give me a drink."
- "Writing is excessive drudgery. It crooks your back, it dims your sight, it twists your stomach and your sides."
- "While I wrote I froze, and what I could not write by the beams of the sun I finished by candlelight."
- "As the harbor is welcome to the sailor, so is the last line to the scribe."

In a contemporary honors thesis, this reflective section offers students the opportunity to discuss the thesis process itself and their personal experience during their thesis work, or to view their thesis in terms of their increasing mastery of the process, the arc of their undergraduate career, or their intellectual development. Hence, in this self-reflection students might describe and analyze their intellectual or creative journey leading to this particular honors project. They might discuss the good and bad choices they made in the course of their thesis work. What did they learn about dealing with primary sources? What do they think they should have done differently? Did they have an effective work plan? What aspects of their work on the thesis project did they find most valuable or rewarding and why? How did they grow as a result of doing the thesis? In other words, the self-reflective section provides an opportunity for students to look back on the highs and lows of their thesis work, to reflect on their preparation and their individual experience of thesis research and writing, and in some cases to address the place of thesis work in their undergraduate career.

A self-reflective section of the thesis also has other aspects to recommend its incorporation as a thesis requirement. It provides students with an opportunity to consider and acknowledge the intellectual guidance and personal support of their thesis advisors. This material is also a valuable step forward into the professional practice of acknowledging the contributions of others. Even if thesis advisors receive some release time or extra pay for their work with thesis students, acknowledgement of their intellectual and personal guidance is especially important for faculty members and their departments. In some honors thesis programs, the honors director or dean takes special pains to ensure that the students' comments are relayed to department chairs and senior administrators at the institution. When an honors director or dean goes out of the way to communicate the good work of faculty advisors, faculty will be even more committed to working with future honors program students.

In addition, some honors programs and colleges ask students completing their thesis to include practical hints or warnings that they think might help other students as they construct their own thesis. When students beginning their thesis work read personal comments by students who have "been there, done that," they perceive the thesis not as a frightening project that will burden their last year of college, but as a rewarding experience, despite its problems, that they, as well as others, truly have the ability to complete. Student comments on their thesis work are often the most credible source for communicating this message.

These reflective comments can also provide important data for program review and assessment. Honors deans and directors can use the self-reflective sections as important documentation of student learning and program satisfaction. During required self-study for accreditation, or whenever the administration is curious about the success of the honors program or college and how students benefit, the comments in a reflective section of the thesis can provide ready-made and credible evidence that would be difficult to obtain in any other way. Moreover, all college and university presidents love to use stories of student success at their institution when talking to prospective students and their parents, to alumni, and to the general public. The personal stories of honors students— of obstacles overcome, of intellectual blossoming, and of superior achievement—*in the students' own words*, culled from their reflective comments, clearly exemplify student success and learning at their highest level at the institution. Honors deans and directors may benefit by sharing these student reflections and personal comments on a regular basis with their administration.

Public Presentation

As we mentioned, one of the distinguishing characteristics of the honors thesis is its public nature, originating in the medieval *disputatio*. Honors programs and colleges still take this oral presentation of thesis work quite seriously. Even though many students make presentations in class or at university research colloquia, most student work is private, between the student and the professor: no one sees the student's work other than the professor. Once the course has ended, it is as if the expiration date has passed: no one looks at a particular piece of student work again, and it is frequently discarded.

In contrast to normal undergraduate work, an honors thesis has an ongoing existence. Honors programs and colleges make completed theses publicly available in a variety of ways. Some honors programs and colleges require an oral thesis defense in front of an audience that may be small (select faculty or by invitation only) or large (the entire academic community or the general public). Instead of a formal thesis defense, other honors programs and colleges require or strongly encourage their students to make a presentation about their thesis at other venues: at the institution's research day or at a similar public forum, at department meetings, at appropriate professional meetings, at the National Conference on Undergraduate Research, to community groups, or at regional and national honors conferences. These regional honors conferences are student-centered and are especially welcoming places for student presentations.

Understandably, some students are anxious about public speaking or insecure about displaying their work publicly; however, public presentation of the honors thesis compels students to take their thesis work seriously and to realize that it is not just another paper. Students usually put more effort into a project that other people will see or hear. Moreover, public presentations, like poster sessions or colloquia, help students develop a different communication skill set and often give them the confidence they previously lacked. This experience may, in fact, be the first time students have had to explain and defend their own ideas in a public setting, something they will likely have to do in graduate or professional studies and in the work world.

Because faculty advisors realize that their names—their imprimatur—will be associated with publicly presented thesis research, they encourage a high level of student performance on the thesis. The honors thesis is clearly more than the product of an individual student's effort: it is the result of a collaboration between student and faculty mentor and reflects not only the quality of the student's work but also the judgment and guidance of the faculty. Consequently, honors theses provide tangible evidence of the quality and diversity of teaching and learning in an honors program and at the institution.

Because undergraduate honors theses are highly valued documents representing outstanding undergraduate achievement at the institution, almost every honors program and college takes pains to archive honors theses so that they will be readily available on campus and to the general public. Such archives, like those for master's and doctoral theses, may be located in the institution's library, in an honors office or lounge for easy student access, or in both locations. Just as research is increasingly carried out online and libraries embrace digital archives, so digital archives of honors theses have supplemented or replaced archives of hard copy or bound theses.

When a thesis archive goes online, the quality of honors work is even more readily accessible to the general public, which is now only a Google away, 24/7, anywhere in the world.

CHAPTER 3

Managing an Honors Thesis Program

SUPPORTING SUCCESSFUL THESIS WORK

Although the primary responsibility for thesis work lies with the student, faculty guidance plays an important role in the success of a thesis. At the same time, a thesis program can also be crucial to the success of a great many thesis students, regardless of how intelligent and capable they are, because students need more than thesis requirements and deadlines. Great students do not automatically produce a great thesies. Experienced honors directors and deans know that bright students can often coast through normal coursework with little effort by cobbling things together at the last minute or by relying on intellect rather than a well-tested work ethic. In thesis work such approaches are a recipe for disaster: an early start and adherence to a carefully developed work plan are likely to have more impact on the success of the thesis than will the student's intellectual ability. Consequently, the best honors programs and colleges carefully structure and manage their thesis programs to prepare their students thoroughly for the thesis, move them into thesis work as early as possible, and assist them in avoiding the pitfalls and overcoming the obstacles that may impede their work.

Thesis work is a new experience for undergraduates, so honors directors, deans, and staff should expect missteps, no matter how prepared students believe they are for the thesis. Many students have trouble understanding that the size and complexity of their thesis project will not allow them to be successful with the haphazard approaches and last-minute scrambles that may have carried the day in past courses, even those with research projects. Left to their own devices, honors students sometimes do not understand or come to terms with the different demands of the thesis until it is too late to do anything about a project that has barely begun or one that has gone seriously awry. Active management, clear guidelines, frequent checkpoints to measure progress, and sometimes active intervention are hallmarks of a good honors thesis program. The rewards of incorporating these strategies can be striking: a high percentage of the honors program students will start their thesis work early; they will make the most of the mentoring relationship with their thesis advisors; and they will finish their thesis on schedule. For these students thesis work will be one of the most valuable experiences in their undergraduate careers.

An honors thesis requires students to take their first steps towards working as independent professionals in their special field of interest. Students who have been highly successful in their other academic work may be surprised at how easily they stumble during this process. Many students discover that they must apply skills that they may not have exercised sufficiently in their previous coursework, e.g., research and writing skills, time management, problem solving, and frequent discussions of central scholarly or creative issues with a faculty member. Inadequacies in these areas lie at the root of almost all unsatisfactory thesis work, from poor writing, disappointing analysis, and inadequate documentation to unacceptable, unfinished, or abandoned theses. Attention must be paid.

Fortunately, honors directors can do much to support students in their thesis work. This chapter will focus on the issues, models, and best strategies that are used in a wide variety of honors thesis programs for the management of thesis work. In many ways an honors director or dean can function like a college athletics director, creating a framework in which individual coaches can lead their players to perform at the highest level possible. The object of honors thesis management is not to take over responsibility for thesis work from students, to co-opt the decision-making process, or to do the heavy lifting for them. Rather, it is to encourage, direct, and support thesis students to make good choices, to both plan and do the hard independent work their thesis will require, to make their thesis work all that it is capable of being, and to perform as students at the highest possible level.

SUPPORTING DIFFERENT KINDS OF THESES

An honors thesis program can improve the success rate of students undertaking thesis work by implementing a variety of measures, from providing written advice addressing common problems to supporting activities for thesis students and their faculty advisors. Many honors thesis programs have incorporated curricular changes, in particular adding a thesis preparation course, as well as additional colloquia or seminars for students engaged in writing a thesis. These efforts will have a significant impact on the effectiveness, satisfaction, and success of all the students undertaking thesis work in an honors program or college despite the diversity of their thesis disciplines and topics. Honors students conducting thesis research in the library, working on an experiment in a college laboratory, or writing a section of the thesis in their rooms will benefit from the sound preparation, focused strategies and advice, and interactions with other thesis students who are part and parcel of most thesis support activities.

The mantra of "individual achievement and independent work" for the honors thesis, however, sometimes makes honors administrators reluctant to provide strong support for thesis students, seeing it as potentially micromanaging thesis work. On the contrary, we would argue that most students actually welcome honors assistance to help them navigate the unknown territory of the honors thesis; they understand that this assistance is intended to give them direction and confidence in their thesis work. Successful programs, whether in athletics or honors, achieve these objectives through frequent interaction with students, carefully monitoring various indicators of student performance, and constantly focusing on students' needs and the areas of the program that warrant improvement. In an honors program, occasionally changing parts of the thesis program or adding new elements to it, which promise improved results, reflect a clear commitment to supporting student performance and success.

One of the ways that honors administrators can manage their thesis programs effectively is to have a thorough understanding of the complete spectrum of student thesis work. Effective management of an honors thesis program requires making provision for the tremendous diversity of areas, topics, and approaches that students can consider in their thesis. But, as discussed in Chapter 2, honors theses also have many features in common even though requirements and expectations vary across disciplines, programs, and institutions. Such commonalities are found not only in the shared approaches and formats for a thesis, but also in the similar problems that students encounter in their thesis work. One useful way to highlight these similarities and shared problems is to look at the disciplinary orientation of the thesis.

The Thesis in the Humanities and Fine Arts

A successful thesis in the humanities and fine arts, like all thesis work, demands that students have the appropriate preparation in their area of special interest; a strong analytical focus—even in the arts, as we will discuss below; a detailed research or creative plan; and the research, documentation, and creative skills necessary for their specific project. At the same time, there are several concerns particular to these disciplines that must be addressed. Many students in the arts and humanities have considerable difficulty selecting a thesis topic and an appropriate thesis advisor. Often they have a wide range of interests in their general discipline, unlike, say, science majors who often become focused on a specific interest early in their academic career. Hence, arts and humanities students may need more faculty direction to move from general interests and a multitude of options for the thesis to a viable and narrower topic.

The most important action that an honors program can undertake is helping these students decide on one option among the many possibilities they are considering rather than obsessing over what would be the "best" thesis topic or project. The desire for an ideal thesis can paralyze students before they even begin their research. They need to pick interesting and doable paths for their research or creative project. A humanities and fine arts student who has trouble selecting a thesis topic should be encouraged to arrange a face-to-face appointment with a potential thesis advisor, or several potential advisors, as early as possible to discuss and settle on a thesis topic or project. In these one-on-one discussions, faculty perspectives and enthusiasm may help to focus and heighten the student's interest in a specific topic or project. Moreover, as a result of such discussions with faculty, the choice of a thesis advisor may become obvious, and the student will have made the transition into actual thesis work almost without realizing it.

In the humanities a thesis may take any number of shapes, but it often closely follows the traditional model for a liberal arts thesis. In their thesis process, most humanities students conduct independent research that is largely confined to library work and focused on the analysis of primary texts, documents, or other scholarly studies. Hence, the humanities thesis is similar to a conventional research paper, blending argument or a new perspective on a subject within the context of research already published. It may focus on historical events, significant individuals, or intellectual and social developments. It may explore philosophical issues; it may examine specific texts or works in order to clarify the ideas of a poet, artist, or thinker; or it may compare and contrast works, artists, and prominent individuals from different periods or in different parts of the world.

In the fine arts, some but not all of a student's thesis work needs to follow the model for research in the humanities. This approach is not always accepted by students contemplating an honors thesis performance, exhibition, or other creative project: convinced that they should work as "artists," they may resist what they see as unnecessary and boring library research. These fine arts students often fixate on their end product, calling on their individual vision and talent to create an artistic work, a dance, a series of paintings, or a play, while ignoring the complex admixture of ideas informing the creative process. They often think of these ideas as simply "theirs," their own unique concept or vision, disregarding the fact that an important part of the artistic process involves thinking about and responding to the ideas and works of others. Quite simply, many undergraduates embrace their own uniqueness despite all evidence to the contrary.

Honors directors and deans can help fine arts students understand the need to examine and contextualize their artistic vision by encouraging them to model themselves on professionals in their fields. A fine arts thesis should be a gateway into both professional quality work and professional concerns. Professional artists expect to be asked about their influences, their intentions, their themes, and their choice of techniques by other artists as well as by the general public. They give media interviews and write requests for grants that cover these same topics. Artists commonly prepare programs for their exhibits or performances that verbally contextualize their work; discuss its themes, vision, or intent; and help the public to understand and appreciate its qualities. Therefore requiring theses in creative areas to contain a substantial written component that addresses these questions is appropriate.

A thesis in the fine arts will benefit from thorough and professional documentation, but documentation of a fine arts thesis may be more diverse than that of a humanities thesis. In some cases multi-media materials can rival the importance of written documentation, and they should be thought of as integral parts of a fine arts thesis. Including a variety of materials, not just printed photos and illustrations, for a fine arts thesis is usually desirable and may include preliminary sketches, stage designs and layouts, production notes highlighting major decisions, interpretative approaches and rationales, and audio or video recordings of discussions with other participants in a thesis performance. Because digital recording and media have provided a wealth of inexpensive possibilities for presenting, explaining, and documenting an artistic work and the artistic process, slide shows, audio and visual files, and other digitized documentation are now commonly included in fine arts theses. As in other disciplines, the fine arts thesis should illustrate an up-to-date mastery of professional concerns and contemporary practices in presentation, documentation, and supplementary materials.

The Thesis in the Social Sciences

The thesis in the social sciences can address any number of issues, but students should be encouraged to start thinking about a thesis topic, or at least a topic area, in their junior year. Most social science theses will require some field or laboratory research, which takes time to develop, execute, analyze, and discuss. For example, much research in the social sciences utilizes surveys. Because students encounter so many surveys in their daily lives (usually badly worded surveys), students often think that a survey or questionnaire is easy to construct. In fact, a well-constructed survey, or any field research or lab study, takes a great deal of time to plan, create, pretest, refine, and then pretest again before it is ready to utilize.

This intricate process is necessary to ensure that the survey is valid and reliable: that it measures what it purports to measure and that its results are consistent through repeated trials. For this reason, students in the social sciences are usually required to take some sort of statistics or research methods course early in pursuit of their major, typically in their sophomore year. Therefore, starting students working on a social science thesis in the junior year is usually desirable because it will require more preparatory work and effort than most students expect.

In addition, since much of the research in the social sciences involves human subjects, social science thesis students must comply with institutional research policies concerning human subjects. Students may have to learn and prove their mastery of institutional research policies. Since this area is complex and involves a number of serious ethical considerations, an early delineation of the thesis project is imperative.

For all these reasons, honors deans and directors should encourage students in the social sciences to think about a thesis topic and connecting with a faculty mentor/advisor as early as is feasible after the methods course in their major.

The Thesis in the Sciences

Like the thesis in the social sciences, the thesis in the sciences generally involves laboratory or fieldwork and often takes an extended period of time to design and complete. Most science students become involved in laboratory or field research early in their course of study, often assisting in faculty research projects and enrolling in research courses, seminars, and independent study projects. Students in the sciences should be encouraged to make early connections with faculty members who are interested in bringing students into their laboratories. Because research in the sciences often has a linear development, students can sometimes use their previous research experience as the basis for similar work in their honors theses.

In addition, faculty members in the sciences who are especially strong and productive often develop excellent mentoring relationships with their students since they have frequent, even daily, contact with students in their labs as well as in the classroom. In fact, as we noted earlier, honors thesis work in the United States first arose in nineteenth-century science departments, which took this mentoring and the desirability of advanced research for their superior students seriously. Such commitment persists today. Contemporary students in the sciences find that their personal experiences in specialized research and their interactions with science faculty usually make the selection of a thesis topic and advisor a fairly straightforward matter. And after the thesis is completed, the strong mentoring relationship between faculty advisor and thesis student frequently continues into an ongoing professional relationship.

Honors directors and thesis administrators should be aware that research (as well as publication) in the sciences often involves unavoidable expenses. Some institutions offer grants to support undergraduate research, but funds are usually limited and early application, often in a student's junior year, is a necessity. For thesis research in the sciences, the honors program or college, as well as the department and the students themselves, may be called on to help cover the laboratory and research expenses. Some honors programs and colleges have found that honors alumni are often enthusiastic supporters of undergraduate research projects and may be generous providers of research support. Alumni are especially sympathetic to the funding needs of students who pursue the same majors they did. On many campuses, however, alumni fundraising can be a sensitive and territorial issue, so institutional approval is usually advisable. These programs of alumni support have been overwhelming successes at some institutions. Such programs clearly strengthen alumni involvement or contacts with the college or university, and, as a result, the total contributions of these benefactors to the institution may actually increase. (For a discussion of alumni fundraising, see Andrews' *Fundrai$ing for Honor$: A Handbook*.)

Finally, honors directors should also be aware that theses in the sciences tend to be shorter than those in the humanities or social sciences, perhaps 20–25 pages in chemistry as compared to 50–75 pages in history. This difference does not reflect less effort by the science students, who have almost certainly spent several terms, if not years, on their projects. It simply means that science theses, like published articles in the sciences, tend to be shorter than those in the humanities or social sciences.

The Pre-Professional Thesis

Some pre-professional programs such as education, engineering, business, architecture, journalism, medicine, and law require extensive work in the field, especially in the student's junior and senior years. Students who have student-teaching, internship, or fieldwork requirements often feel that completing a thesis as well will be overwhelming: they have neither the time nor the energy to do everything. Moreover, internships are extremely popular now, and many students believe that practical work in their field will be of greater value than the library work associated with the traditional honors thesis. They may also see internships and other hands-on programs of study and training as less stressful and, frankly, as more fun than an honors thesis. As a consequence, many students in this situation are tempted to decide not to do an honors thesis, even if this decision means that they will fail to complete their honors program or college requirements. Such situations have become conspicuous stress points in many honors programs and colleges, with significant consequences for program success.

Honors deans and directors should address this problem by helping these students see that they are not facing an either/or situation, that the honor thesis is both valuable and possible for them. After all, the traditional thesis was intended to bring the skills and learning acquired throughout the student's entire academic career to bear in a specialized capstone project. The types of learning included in the college experience have clearly expanded in recent years through the inclusion of off-campus programs, just as many students' academic careers have extended over a longer period and across several institutions. But having the thesis function as the final integrative element in an undergraduate's career remains a possibility: it just needs a little help.

Some honors programs have successfully incorporated pre-professional experiences into their thesis programs. Perhaps the most important thing an honors director can do is discuss with students early on how such off-campus study and work can be used in a thesis. (See Gustafson and Cureton, 2014.) This conversation allows students to envision the internship or other experience in a way that grounds and supplements their later thesis work. Pre-professional students can then create a sound honors thesis that makes significant use of their fieldwork or other pre-professional experience.

Another critical step is for the honors director or dean to put the student in contact with a sympathetic advisor. Because many academic faculty may not be familiar with a nontraditional thesis based on internships or fieldwork, the honors administrator may need to help students find a thesis advisor who is willing to help them incorporate field experiences, foreign study, or internships into their thesis work. Sometimes finding an appropriate thesis advisor and thesis topic will require flexibility in a number of areas. A business major who has an internship in marketing may find a thesis focusing on the effectiveness of financial incentives for marketing staff, under the direction of a supportive psychology professor, to be an interesting thesis project that would make good use of the internship experience.

It seems reasonable to assume that in the near future internships will become common parts of the undergraduate experience. As new faculty who have themselves also had valuable internships and other extra-academic experiences join the academy, the blending of off-campus work with traditional thesis research will become normalized. But until then, honors administrators will sometimes need to take the initiative in making it possible for students to do an honors thesis incorporating internships and other off-campus experiences.

The Interdisciplinary Thesis

Since the late twentieth century, interdisciplinary study has become increasingly common in higher education, but it also raises some potential problems for thesis work. On the one hand, some honors programs and colleges encourage interdisciplinary study in their course offerings and may even require an interdisciplinary thesis for the student's capstone, integrating the students' variety of experiences. Moreover, many honors students have a variety of interests that they would like to follow in their thesis work. Students with double majors or a major and one or more minors often want to incorporate the content and approaches from several of these disciplines into their thesis work.

At the same time, an interdisciplinary thesis can easily run into problems in an academic setting that is tightly organized along disciplinary and departmental lines. Interdisciplinary theses usually require more than one faculty advisor, and these advisors bring with them different methodologies, expectations, and concerns that need coordination to ensure that the student receives clear and consistent direction. Furthermore, assigning more than one faculty advisor to a thesis student can sometimes lead to administrative complications, especially related to faculty workload and the assignment of release credit or financial compensation to faculty for their thesis-advising commitment.

Some honors programs and colleges are reluctant to encourage interdisciplinary theses because of the potential problems outlined above, the complexity of their management, but most of all because of the increased commitment of faculty advisors required for interdisciplinary theses. Finding just one faculty advisor for a thesis is often a difficult task; unearthing even more advisors can seem Herculean. On the other hand, some people in honors programs and colleges are convinced that the educational value of interdisciplinary thesis work outweighs its drawbacks for both students and faculty. Ultimately, an honors administrator must decide to what extent interdisciplinary thesis work fits other aspects of the institution's honors program or college and the extent to which their thesis program can support it successfully.

THE THESIS COURSE AND CREDITS

Honors programs and colleges normally require all students completing an honors thesis to register the thesis as a course for credit. The traditional or liberal arts thesis was connected to a single 3–4-credit course taken in a student's senior year, the time when the majority of the research and writing was completed. Today, however, a great deal of variation exists among colleges and universities about when students start the thesis work and register for thesis credit and even the total number of credits students receive for their thesis work. At first glance, these differences can appear not only confusing but troubling. Why does a student at one institution register for a 1-credit thesis, while at another institution a student writes a 6–12-credit thesis spread over two years? Do such radical differences exist in our academic world concerning the scope and quality required for an honors thesis? What are the best strategies for assigning credits for thesis work?

At some institutions the number of credits awarded for an honors thesis depends upon the length and scope of the thesis: the longer the thesis, the more credits given. At many institutions, however, the number of credits awarded for thesis work seems to have less to do with the scope and quality expected for an honors thesis than it does with the structuring of thesis work at the institution and especially the extent to which thesis preparatory coursework and ancillary activities are a required part of the thesis process. The most influential determinants for total thesis credits are the number of semesters or quarters during which some type of registered thesis work takes place and whether such thesis work is indicated by just one course or by several different courses for different aspects of thesis work. These credits may accrue from a thesis preparation course, a thesis research course, a thesis writing course, or a supplemental honors thesis course taken in conjunction with a non-honors departmental thesis course.

The Single-Course Thesis

At most institutions the thesis is linked to the traditional single "honors thesis" course, the 3–4-credit basic unit of academic study, and is registered either in a department or in the honors program or college. As such it resembles an independent research course culminating in a research paper. The honors thesis course, however, has higher base-line expectations that differentiate it from other research work. As already noted, an honors thesis is typically longer, more complex, more rigorous, and more significant than a normal undergraduate research project completed for a regular course or for an independent study devised by the student.

Identifying the honors thesis as a single course has many advantages. It defines the scope of thesis work appropriate for undergraduates: larger than a research paper that is part of a normal course, yet smaller than a master's thesis but heading in that direction. Because both students and faculty are familiar with the amount of work in a normal college course and with the quality of work required from students in it, framing the honors thesis as a 3–4-credit project allows them to have a general understanding of the amount of work expected for an honors thesis, even as they adjust it for "honors quality" work. Furthermore, the 3–4-credit thesis course easily fits into most students' schedules and is consistent with departmental research projects. For students who are trying to pack as much as possible into the junior and senior years, a 3–4-credit thesis does not seriously limit the other upper-division courses that they can take, nor does it rule out participation in overseas study or internships.

Finally, the one-course model for the honors thesis can be helpful when things go badly: if a student does not complete a thesis—and it does happen—it affects only 3–4 credits in an undergraduate's total career. When a student's thesis work is inadequate or unfinished because of illness or other valid reasons, a single thesis course is not likely to stop a student from graduating. When such crises occur, the honors director or dean may be able to work with the thesis advisors to complete a late-withdrawal from the thesis course, reduce the number of credits the student receives for the thesis course, or even downgrade it to a conventional independent study course.

Furthermore, students often need or receive extra time for their thesis work, but when these problems arise during the last term of an undergraduate's career, the situation becomes especially problematic. While most students finish incomplete work in a week or two, a few students make repeated requests for more time; others just leave campus, abandoning the thesis and losing contact with the thesis advisor as well as the honors dean or director. Unless a faculty member intervenes, most institutions automatically change an Incomplete to a failing grade after a few months. Although some students may mistakenly believe that thesis work is a dispensable part of their undergraduate career, failing the thesis course can have shocking consequences. In some cases failing to pass the thesis course may result in the failure to satisfy all graduation requirements, not just those for the honors program or honors college. Simply put, no thesis can mean no degree. This situation is painful not only for students but also for honors administrators and faculty dedicated to helping their students succeed. While few options exist at this stage, a 3–4-credit thesis course may facilitate solutions.

The Extended Thesis Course

Some honors programs and colleges require an extensive thesis course, perhaps accounting for as many as 6–12 credits, that combines preparatory exercises and other assignments with thesis research and writing. This course may be offered as one large course in the student's final year, or, more commonly, separated into a two-course sequence. Such a two-course sequence essentially incorporates what other institutions may offer as separate thesis preparation and thesis writing courses. (For a detailed discussion of the thesis preparation course, see Chapter 4.) Hence, the extended thesis course includes not just thesis research and writing, but a wide variety of activities:

- reading a sampling of completed honors theses at the institution;
- library-centered instruction and activities;
- focused research projects and bibliographic exercises;
- critiquing past or present thesis work;
- discussions with students who have completed a thesis;
- preparation for an oral presentation or a defense of the thesis.

Whether the extended thesis course starts in the junior year and finishes in the senior year or is taken as a unit during the senior year, the additional credits are typically related to the activities that lead to or supplement thesis research, writing, and presentation.

The extended thesis course presses home to students the fact that honors thesis work is a much bigger project than a research paper for a regular course, that it demands a larger commitment of time and work, and that preparation and planning for the thesis are integral components necessary for its successful completion. It also provides an umbrella for other desirable activities: mentoring of thesis students by student peers who are further along in the thesis process; the honing of research skills and bibliographic conventions; and ongoing interactions among thesis students sharing their experiences, achievements, and problems in the thesis process.

At a few institutions, the extended thesis course is taught on a tutorial basis by thesis advisors, and the credits assigned to it give faculty greater recognition for their work with thesis students. Other honors programs and colleges see real value in combining both classroom and tutorial instruction for thesis work. At large institutions, students from a single department or students with related thesis projects can be brought together as a group in the early stages of their thesis work for instruction from an appropriate faculty member before splitting off for intensive work under the direction of their specific thesis advisor. In such cases, students receive focused instruction from experts, and participating departments and programs receive additional recognition for their work with thesis students.

At many institutions, the honors director, dean, staff, or dedicated faculty may teach the preparatory, non-discipline-specific parts of the extended thesis course. As the course continues, it can be structured so that the number of general class meetings decreases as students increasingly meet with their thesis advisors and work under their direction. Required submission of exercises, preliminary bibliographies, early drafts, and reports can replace the need for some class meetings and are appropriate for the students' increasingly independent work. Nonetheless, a few group meetings of thesis students and the honors administrator or appropriate faculty advisors are helpful to ensure satisfactory progress and provide support for the students. Students find great value in discussing the activities, progress, and problems of individual thesis projects with other students, as well as with the honors director or dean, even after the thesis is well underway.

Variable Credits for Thesis Work

While many honors programs and colleges require that every thesis be registered for the same number of credits regardless of length or subject, other honors programs and colleges allow students to register their theses for a differing number of credits, such as 1–6 credits or 6–12 credits. The options provided by variable credits accommodate larger thesis projects and also provide a way to assign fewer credits when necessary in special circumstances, even though the majority of students may register for the conventional 3–4-credit hours of thesis work. Special financial constraints or limits on the maximum number of credits allowed per term, as discussed previously, may make a 1–2-credit thesis course a desirable or necessary option for some students. In other cases, an honors program or college may wish to pair a 1–3-credit honors thesis course with a departmental thesis course for a total of 4–6 credits. Or a student may have completed a large research project with a faculty member, and the 1–2-credit hours for the honors thesis course reflect just the extra work needed to turn this project into an honors thesis. In all of these cases, the added honors thesis course clearly indicates on the transcript that the student completed honors-level thesis work.

Flexibility in the number of credits given for a thesis should not undermine the standards or requirements for the honors thesis. Honors programs and colleges must have a credit policy for the thesis that is consistent as well as flexible, and honors directors and deans need to make sure that this policy is clearly understood by both students and faculty advisors. Variable credit options should be used rarely and only for special circumstances so that the honors thesis retains a conceptual consistency. For this reason, both the honors administrator and the thesis advisor need to be involved in any deviation from the normal number of credits allocated to a thesis. Moreover, the issue of the appropriate credits for a specific thesis project needs to be factored into the thesis proposal. Adjusting the thesis project or the credits it will receive at the start of the process is always preferable to struggling at the end of a term to determine how many credits a completed thesis is worth.

Faculty advisors have the clear responsibility for determining the scope of the thesis project and the acceptability of an honors thesis within the standards of their discipline, as well as for determining the thesis course grade. But just as clearly, the number of credits assigned to an honors thesis must conform to institutional standards as overseen by the honors director or dean. In fact, thesis advisors often tell honors administrators that they are glad to have a clear and consistent policy on thesis credits because it relieves them of having to make murky and perhaps arbitrary decisions that one thesis is worth 3 credits while another might be worth 4 credits or more. Moreover, when the scope of the thesis is clear and consistent, more students are likely to undertake and then complete their thesis project on schedule because they neither underestimate nor overestimate the work expected of them.

COMMUNICATING THESIS EXPECTATIONS

Successful thesis administrators understand that thesis work cannot flourish in the dark. The entire academic community needs to be aware that the honors thesis is an important part of undergraduate work at the college or university and that many outstanding students are working on and completing a thesis. All administrators, faculty, and staff at the institution should have a basic understanding of student eligibility for honors thesis work and the nature of thesis projects, just as they all should understand the institution's general education requirements. In addition, they should understand the role of faculty mentoring in thesis work and any special aspects of thesis work such as public presentations and honors recognitions. Informed faculty are an invaluable part of an institution's commitment to supporting honors thesis work.

Honors deans and directors must take primary responsibility for establishing uniform thesis procedures at their institutions. If thesis projects operate on an *ad hoc* basis, wide variation in practices can easily develop. While this may be acceptable in some departmental courses, it is not appropriate in an honors thesis program. Inexplicable differences in standards for the honors thesis can easily undermine the integrity and attractiveness of a thesis program. Honors students will soon learn that Professor Friendly accepted a sloppy 17-page English thesis with no bibliography from student Jane Doe, while John Jones' advisor required him to complete an impeccably researched 85-page history thesis, the equivalent of an MA thesis. Even worse, in this context, many students may believe the rumor that another student was given an A for the thesis course despite never completing the thesis.

Thesis work is highly individualized and needs to be. Even though individual students will be engaged in independent work on specialized thesis projects, and a wide variety of faculty will be evaluating this thesis work, it is critical that students and others in the academic community trust that all honors theses are treated fairly and equitably throughout the institution. Just as in lower-division honors courses, students fear the possibility of having to meet excessively high standards and resent doing rigorous and extensive work, no matter how valuable, if they believe that other students in similar situations are required to do much less. Therefore, clear communication and effective communication paths are essential for any successful thesis program. Everyone recognizes the difficulty of defining the honors thesis. But an honors administrator needs to set the parameters: both students and faculty need a clear explanation of thesis expectations, consistent requirements and procedures for thesis work, and an indication of the shared standards for thesis work. Repeated dissemination of such information can do much to encourage equivalent standards across diverse disciplines and ensure that both students and faculty understand the work that will be expected of them.

Providing Thesis Information to Students

The honors thesis is a new experience for students, and they need a detailed explanation of what the thesis is and what will be required of them, as well as practical advice on central aspects of thesis work. This information is a critical factor in the success of all thesis programs. Many honors programs and colleges provide potential thesis students with such information starting as early as the sophomore year. This information can be disseminated in lower-division honors courses or special meetings of honors students, as well as through handouts, the honors website, emails, or a thesis preparation course.

The following list of crucial information and advice may be useful:

- A basic overview of the thesis and common expectations for its scope, length, and quality.

- Required format, including documentation requirements, reflective comments, and any other special sections for the thesis.

- Forms that need to be completed during the thesis process: identification of thesis advisor(s), formal registration of individual thesis projects, progress reports, arrangements for the public presentation of thesis work, approval form for completed theses, honors senior checkout and exit evaluation.

- Advice on finding a thesis advisor.

- Advice on selecting a thesis topic.

- Opportunities and deadlines for financial support of thesis work.

- Deadlines for submission of the formal thesis proposal and the final draft to the thesis advisor(s), for honors program or college approval, and for archiving.

- Requirements and opportunities for presenting thesis research locally, regionally, and nationally.

Honors deans and directors should supplement this basic information and advice in many areas. Experienced honors administrators acknowledge and respond to the realities of honors thesis work as well as to its ideals. Although thesis students have been at the college or university for several years, they still vary widely in their skills, preparation, and work habits. Not all students, no matter how smart or well-versed in their discipline, no matter how high their SAT scores or college GPA, come to their honors thesis work perfectly prepared and in possession of all the skills that they will need for their work. Having the potential to create a superior honors thesis is not the same thing as being adequately prepared for it.

Furthermore, students may have serious holes in their knowledge of campus resources, research regulations, and professional practices. In particular, they may not understand the extent of the college library's local holdings, its standard services such as online access to other materials and interlibrary loan, or the special privileges it may give to thesis students such as private carrels or extended borrowing periods. Most students do not know that their school has a human subjects review committee or that they may be responsible for research or laboratory expenses. In addition, many students are not particularly good at scheduling or planning, especially for work that may extend over two, three, or four semesters. And even after years of study, some have no idea how to approach a potential thesis advisor or talk to a faculty member outside the classroom.

Good faculty advisors will encourage their thesis students to address and work through their weaknesses over the course of their thesis work, but successful thesis programs try to decrease this burden on faculty advisors. In particular, they can use their lower-division courses and thesis preparation courses to help students develop the analytical and writing skills they will need in their thesis work and introduce them to successful research practices. Because honors programs have a strong role in structuring a student's undergraduate career, they can use honors coursework, thesis requirements, workshops, and deadlines to guide students onto paths that will lead towards a successful conclusion to their thesis work.

Providing Thesis Information to Faculty Advisors

Honors administrators also need to communicate information about the honors thesis directly to faculty advisors. These faculty need basically the same information that students need: deadlines, forms, format requirements, opportunities for presenting the research, and opportunities for financial support of thesis work. Faculty advisors are sometimes the most appreciative audience for advice on the best strategies for engaging in thesis work even if this advice is ostensibly intended for students. Other information, such as an overview of effective mentoring practices, may be targeted specifically at faculty advisors and will be of particular value to new faculty and first-time thesis advisors. Most faculty welcome support and suggestions from the honors program or college, either through direct contact with the honors director and staff or through written materials. Such materials should be readily accessible online as well as distributed in hard copy because faculty may need to refresh their memories about deadlines, forms, and other protocols.

The following list highlights information particularly relevant to faculty thesis advisors:

- Advice on helping students select and focus their thesis interests on a specific topic that is appropriate for an advanced undergraduate and that can be completed by the submission deadline.

- Advice on helping the student establish a thesis work schedule, including meeting times with the thesis advisor and plans for submission of drafts.

- Advice on the degree of involvement necessary by both the thesis advisor and others for the completion of a successful honors thesis.

- Advice on handling in a timely manner any serious problems or conflicts that may arise.

- Information on the thesis advisor's responsibilities in the approval and grading processes for the thesis.

- Information about the involvement of the honors program or college in the approval and grading process for the thesis.

- Information about faculty involvement in any formal presentation of the thesis or in honors ceremonies.

ENCOURAGING AN EARLY START ON THE THESIS

Successful honors thesis programs stack the odds in their favor and perhaps take inspiration from the apocryphal Chicago model for voting: do it early and often. Well-managed thesis programs often introduce students to the prospect of the honors thesis at the beginning of their college careers, and they help students develop and hone the skills they will need in thesis work. Although many normal undergraduate courses may neglect independent analysis and research, lower-division honors courses generally emphasize critical thinking and writing, focused research assignments, class presentations, and formal papers. Activities of this type clearly prepare the way for undertaking comparable activities in later thesis projects. Honors programs and colleges often offer a junior-year thesis preparation course that is explicitly designed to jump-start a thesis project, and shrewd honors programs and colleges strongly encourage their students to participate in departmental research projects and/or enroll in research courses as well as to take advanced courses in areas of their discipline that are of particular interest to them.

In addition, honors faculty and current thesis students can showcase the honors thesis in a way that will have a strong impact on lower-division students. In their classes and discussions with first- and second-year students, honors faculty and staff should refer to the thesis projects of previous students or bring up the connection between their current coursework and recent honors theses that may be related to it. Moreover, arranging for current thesis students to come into a lower-division class to discuss their thesis project, or having a panel of thesis students discuss their research methods in conjunction with a course research project, brings thesis work vividly to life. It also breaks down the separation between upper- and lower-division study, between freshman/sophomores and seniors, while fostering the idea that the thesis is the natural end point in an honors student's academic career. In these ways and many others, successful honors programs and colleges go beyond just offering or requiring a thesis: they *guide* students towards honors thesis work from their earliest days on campus.

On the subject of starting early, we leave you with the words of the novelist David Foster Wallace, who completed not one but two honors theses—one in philosophy and one in creative writing. Of his thesis work he wrote, "The trick was starting early, in September instead of February. I'd watched several friends put themselves through hell the year before by futzing around the first semester, so I started early, and it wasn't that hard" (Wallace, 1999).

STARTING THESIS WORK IN THE JUNIOR YEAR

The majority of honors programs and colleges require or at least strongly encourage students to begin the early stages of their actual thesis work by their junior year: thinking about a topic, securing advisors, preparing an outline, working out a research plan, and sketching a timetable. This is the ideal time to start work on a specific thesis because students have already decided on their majors and are taking advanced courses in their disciplines. In addition, they have a clear view of the requirements in their majors as well a rough idea of other interesting opportunities for study or internships on and off campus. These third-year students have only a few semesters remaining before graduation, but they still have enough time to accommodate most of their academic needs and desires through careful scheduling.

The senior year is often too late for some students to begin thesis work although most students do the major part of their thesis research or creative work in their senior year. The days are long past when a student could easily complete a traditional senior thesis in the liberal arts following a "junior year abroad," still a common feature at many liberal arts colleges. In the current academic world, if the student delays preparation and early work on the thesis until the senior year, some projects are no longer viable, deadlines for applying for research funds have past, faculty may resist last-minute requests to become thesis advisors, and conflicts in programs and courses can scuttle the thesis work of even the finest honors students. Consequently, most honors programs and colleges have dropped the misleading term "senior thesis" and typically refer to the undergraduate honors thesis as the honors project, the capstone project, or simply the honors thesis.

Requiring a junior-year start to honors thesis work also alerts students to the fact that thesis work will be significantly different than their previous academic work. Although students recognize that the thesis is a large and complex project that may require more planning and work than they have previously undertaken, they have real difficulty recognizing that a senior-year honors thesis needs to be started as much as a year in advance. Many honors programs and colleges have found that simply telling students to start thesis work as early as possible or addressing the necessity for an early choice of thesis topic and advisor in honors program publications is not effective. Procrastination is common at all levels of the academic world; honors students have often ignored good advice and done just fine, and some students are convinced that they really can do all their thesis work in just a few weeks.

Furthermore, their other courses have conditioned them to think in one-semester or one-quarter increments, to believe that coursework cannot begin until they are registered for the course, and to assume that research projects are started after the beginning of the course. Therefore, many honors programs and colleges have adopted junior-year requirements that move students into thesis work before the final year of college, dispelling many of these misconceptions and alerting students to the fact that they cannot approach thesis work as they have their previous research projects: waiting till the eleventh hour.

This guided start can be as simple as requiring registration for the thesis project and the selection of a faculty advisor in the student's junior year. The choice of a thesis project and a faculty advisor are not ironclad decisions: they can always be changed later as necessary. Students need to know that if their interests change or if their initial project does not seem likely to succeed, their junior-year start will give them time to modify it, or even switch to another project and faculty advisor. In some honors programs and colleges, these junior-year requirements may be expanded to include the submission of a thesis work plan, a preliminary bibliography for research, and even first drafts of an early section of the thesis. Most commonly, however, honors programs and colleges introduce a required junior-year thesis preparation course that includes such activities. (See Chapter 4 for a full discussion of these courses.)

THE RELATIONSHIP BETWEEN THESIS WORK AND ATTRITION

Improving the retention of third- and fourth-year students in the honors program or college is an important consideration. At many institutions around the country, students fail to finish the honors program or fail to graduate from an honors college because they drift away from honors work after their sophomore year. Honors coursework frequently parallels an institution's general education requirements; hence, honors students finish most of their lower-division honors coursework by the end of the sophomore year. Honors students who enter with Advanced Placement credits or other college credits may finish their lower-division requirements even sooner. Without the connection of taking honors courses, students can lose close contact with honors faculty, advisors, staff, and the community of other honors students as they concentrate on their majors, focus on possible career paths, and pursue other interests and commitments, both on and off campus. Left to themselves, a troubling number of students realize too late that they will be unable to fit their thesis work into an already crammed final-year schedule. At this point, many in this group abandon the idea of doing a thesis and drop out of honors.

Much upper-division attrition in an honors program or college is the result of students' failure to complete the honors thesis. This can sometimes raise difficult questions about the thesis. Can a good honors program or college eliminate the thesis requirement? Could a re-conceptualization of thesis work both maintain honors standards and improve retention in the program? Could adjustments in the current thesis program improve success rates? All of the honors directors and deans we contacted lamented the fact that too few students, including some of their best students, completed an honors thesis. Some honors programs and colleges have addressed this problem by making the honors thesis an option rather than a requirement or by adjusting the scope and nature of the thesis. As we mentioned earlier, some honors directors and deans are making strong efforts to include new disciplines, new learning experiences, and non-traditional materials and approaches into thesis work.

The overwhelming majority of honors programs and colleges, however, have addressed the problem of senior attrition by adjusting and restructuring their thesis programs. Most honors deans and directors see increased student involvement with honors, including during the last two years of college, as the key to lowering attrition. They have focused their efforts on keeping students involved in honors work and associating with other students on the same path. Many of these honors directors and deans recognize that the honors thesis is not simply part of the problem—"It's too hard," "It doesn't fit in with my other coursework," "How will it help me get a job?" "It's too late do a thesis now"—but that it can be part of the solution.

Thesis work can provide the underpinning for superior upper-division study, providing a developmental path and a series of ongoing interactions that can improve honors retention. Some aspects of thesis work that may on the surface appear to be problematic, especially the size and duration of the thesis project, can actually strengthen an honors program and improve retention. Because a thesis is a big project optimally started in the junior year, junior-year requirements and a thesis preparation course can provide an effective transition between lower-division and upper-division honors work. Moreover, as Richard J. Light (2004) points out, promoting early contacts with a thesis advisor can result in a long-term relationship between student and faculty that often becomes the highlight of a student's undergraduate career. The honors director or dean should help students understand that the thesis project *is* doable, *does* connect with other coursework, and *is* a tangible product that can be shown to potential employers, often serving as a demonstration of independent achievement that is highly valued by both graduate schools and employers.

The emphasis on junior-year work on the honors thesis can assume a variety of forms. Several honors programs and colleges have attempted to move the bulk of the thesis work into the junior year, directly continuing the momentum of honors work from the second year into the third and leaving the senior year open for spill-over thesis work. A few others have designed the thesis course as a two-semester sequence of equally weighted thesis-related courses, starting in either the junior year or the first semester of the senior year. Many honors programs and colleges, however, have introduced a required junior-year thesis preparation course with the clear objectives of increasing the number of students who start a thesis, raising the thesis completion rate, and improving general thesis quality. The thesis preparation course does not appear to require a significant commitment from students, especially when it is a 1-credit offering, yet it can be very effective in motivating students to break their inertia about thesis work, bringing them into early contact with thesis advisors, and lighting the spark of independent research in their minds. (Chapter 4 will present a full discussion of the rationale, approaches, and models for the thesis preparation course.)

SELECTING A THESIS TOPIC AND ADVISOR

The two most challenging tasks for thesis-bound students are selecting a thesis advisor and deciding on an appropriate thesis topic. Students are used to choosing from fixed courses with assigned instructors; they believe that choosing a thesis topic and advisor is a similar process, and many assume that once they have chosen a specific topic, they simply need to sign up a faculty member to grade it, just as they might do with an independent study course. On the other hand, they are just as likely to overthink and agonize about picking a topic and advisor. Left to their own devices, students may easily get stuck in the selection process, have great difficulty settling on a thesis topic, put off the selection of a thesis advisor, or give up on the thesis itself when they encounter difficulties. Consequently, many honors programs and colleges take pains to explain that this selection process is not a matter of straightforward choices like choosing a meal in a cafeteria. It is more like preparing a meal on one's own, and students will be well advised to seek early contact with a faculty member who has experience in cooking up research projects. Moreover, students should be cautioned that they need to have options and backup plans for their thesis work and may need to make many adjustments along the way.

Although some students may have already developed a working relationship with a potential thesis advisor, most have not. They may have taken several courses from the same professor, may feel some sort of intellectual connection with one faculty member or another, but are still reluctant to approach that person to be a thesis advisor. Outside a normal classroom situation, many students are intimidated by their professors and are afraid that their ideas may seem stupid. In addition, students sometimes face the task of approaching faculty they barely know: having to make a cold call intimidates even self-confident students. Moreover, the possibility always exists that if a student does find and contact someone who appears to be the perfect advisor for a thesis, the student may still face insurmountable obstacles: the potential advisor may be scheduled for a sabbatical or leave of absence, too busy to take on a thesis student, no longer interested in the topic, or reluctant to work with a student whom the professor may be meeting for the first time.

Honors directors and deans need to help students see that the selection of a thesis topic and an advisor are interlocking in an inherently give-and-take process. The choice of a faculty advisor defines the type of thesis project a student can pursue, and the choice of a thesis topic by the student usually leads to only a handful of faculty with expertise in that area. Moreover, the selection process is often not quick and easy. Students frequently must adjust or compromise when choosing either their topic or their faculty advisor. Some students may encounter a dead end, forcing them to resort to Plan B or even Plan C for their thesis topic and advisor. Students interested in working with a particular faculty member may need to adjust their topic to fit the advisor's specialized interests or even abandon their initial ideas for an interesting topic that the faculty advisor suggests. Furthermore, students determined to pursue a highly specialized or unusual topic may need some time, and even the help of the honors director or dean, to find the right advisor.

Honors administrators who wish to help their students avoid bottlenecks and other problems in the selection of the thesis project and faculty advisor should encourage students to make direct contact with potential advisors as early as possible, even if the student is uncertain about the choice of a thesis topic. Faculty advice carries great weight, and successful theses usually need strong faculty input and direction from the start. For example, faculty can help students see that the initial idea for a thesis needs to be narrowed or that another research approach may be more appealing and viable. Moreover, the student's initial draft of the thesis proposal may require much discussion and multiple rewrites that the faculty advisor will want to oversee. Honors directors and deans can help to convince students that these changes are refinements, not setbacks, which will enable them to be even more successful at their thesis work.

The expertise of faculty advisors and the personal relationships with their thesis students will have an inspirational and productive impact on the students' thesis work. The thesis becomes more than just the student's project; it becomes something in which both the faculty advisor and the student are heavily invested. Thus, when the faculty advisor asks the student for a detailed outline of the student's research plans or a proposed schedule of meetings, the student will feel that this process is normal rather than an onerous outside requirement imposed by the honors program or college. Even if the advisor suggests that the student needs additional coursework for a successful thesis, the student usually accedes with little or no complaint (and students in their junior year still have time to adjust future course schedules). Because thesis work requires a deeper and more complex relationship between student and faculty than is usually present in the classroom situation, early identification of an advisor also provides the time for a productive mentoring relationship to develop.

Tenure-Track Faculty and Other Thesis Advisors

Most honors programs and colleges require students to have a full-time tenure-track faculty advisor for the honors thesis. But students today may have a harder time than in the past finding even one tenure-track faculty member to serve as a thesis advisor. Because colleges and universities increasingly rely on part-timers, adjuncts, non-tenure track faculty appointments, graduate students, and even undergraduates for instruction, student contact with tenure-track faculty has significantly decreased in recent years at some institutions.

In addition to the shrinking number of tenure-track faculty is the issue of whether the thesis advisor needs to be a tenure-track faculty member at all. Sometimes the selection of non-tenure-track advisors becomes a necessary option, especially when the thesis incorporates student teaching, overseas study, or internship experiences. Furthermore, work that decades ago was assigned only to tenure-track faculty, such as advising or field and laboratory supervision, is currently spread among a variety of "specialists" in the academic world. Without question, some non-tenured faculty and staff can be excellent thesis advisors, and restricting such mentoring possibilities may appear to be a bit out of touch and excessively concerned with academic status.

At the same time, many honors programs and colleges have serious concerns about using non-tenure-track instructors, staff, adjuncts, and temporary appointments as thesis advisors. At most institutions their work is narrowly defined, and thesis student mentoring lies outside their contractual responsibilities. Non-tenure-track instructors are normally not paid for work outside their direct instructional responsibilities; thus they are often not expected or even allowed to serve on department or college committees, to vote at department meetings, or to take on departmental or institutional advisement tasks. In addition, some have neither the academic qualifications, a substantial professional or research background, or the years of teaching and advisement experience that their tenure-track colleagues possess. Because their connection with the college or university is *ad hoc* or temporary, adjunct or term-to-term faculty may have uncertain futures at the institution and consequently less commitment to the institution and the extra work required of an honors thesis advisor. In fact, those adjuncts may not even be available the following year when the student will most need the faculty advisor.

Furthermore, when problems arise with the non-tenure-track advisor's work, an honors administrator can bring little institutional pressure to bear to resolve matters. Therefore, most honors programs and colleges carefully weigh the advantages and risks of using non-tenure-track thesis advisors and make decisions on a case-by-case basis. When the qualifications of such an advisor are of concern, having a tenure-track faculty member working with the student in a secondary role, in a sense operating as an institutional backup, may be desirable.

One or More Thesis Advisors

Requiring only a single thesis advisor, whether tenure-track or not, has some undeniable advantages. It offers a clear and uncomplicated model for mentoring activities. Both students and faculty advisors understand their roles: everything is straightforward, from scheduling meetings and reading drafts to suggesting revisions and grading the completed thesis. The student has only one set of suggestions to follow, one advisor to please. Moreover, one advisor reduces the administrative complexities related to faculty workload. A single faculty advisor can easily receive credit for mentoring work required in a thesis project, clearly reducing accounting problems at institutions where faculty thesis advisors receive supplemental pay or where thesis advisement work can accrue toward release or reassigned time.

The disadvantages of having only one thesis advisor are equally clear, especially when a thesis advisor does not perform well. If the advisor cancels meetings, shows little interest in the student's work, or is inadequate in other ways, the thesis student will not receive the guidance or support needed and expected. For a student intent on getting the most out of the thesis experience or who needs assistance and encouragement to overcome difficulties, one may very well be the loneliest number. Furthermore, the academic community believes strongly that there is an institutional commitment, even a legal responsibility, to provide good faculty mentoring for student thesis work. Hence, multiple advisors can offer some protection for both the student and the institution.

Some honors programs and colleges require two or even three thesis advisors, and a few have a committee responsible for advising and evaluating the honors thesis at one stage or another. One important reason frequently cited for such requirements is that the involvement of several faculty members in the student's thesis work furthers the institution's conception of and commitment to the thesis and the honors program or college. For some institutions, the honors thesis is the capstone not merely of the student's honors program or honors college but of the student's entire undergraduate career, including the study of diverse areas that have made an important contribution to the student's thesis work: requiring multiple advisors embraces this diversity. At some liberal arts colleges, faculty consider such participation a normal part of their academic responsibility. Other honors programs and colleges believe that requiring multiple advisors for thesis work is the right fit for their unique emphasis on interdisciplinary study in earlier honors coursework. For these honors programs and colleges, the advantages of multiple faculty advisors outweigh the difficulties such a requirement may introduce into thesis work.

Working with several advisors normally presents more challenges for students than working with only one, but there are benefits as well. Certainly, scheduling meetings becomes more difficult; more people need to be satisfied, and more egos will need tending. But learning to deal with these contingencies may ultimately be one of the most valuable parts of the thesis experience for some students. Just as importantly, at the intellectual level, having multiple advisors offers many advantages. Each advisor brings a different perspective to the thesis project, new ideas, new questions, new suggestions, all of which help students weigh one idea or approach against another, forcing them to examine problems from multiple perspectives and stretch themselves in their thesis work. Multiple advisors underscore the notion that advanced thesis research and creative projects are an evolving dialogue not just with one authority but with many, whether in on-campus discussions or through research using printed books, articles, and other media.

At the practical level, each advisor can provide helpful assistance. A second advisor can clarify the concerns of the first advisor, emphasize other aspects of the thesis work such as creating and refining an effective work plan, or just provide added intellectual and emotional support for the student. Thus, a second or third advisor offers backup for the main advisor in whatever way is necessary.

If the primary mentoring relationship encounters difficulties for one reason or another, the second or third advisor can assume the role of primary thesis advisor and secure any necessary assistance from other faculty. Resolving problems in thesis advisement at the faculty level rather than through the intervention of the honors director or dean is always best. Using multiple advisors makes this possible.

When an institution requires multiple advisors or provides an option for multiple advisors, the advisors' disciplines are often the major consideration. An English major studying the influence of Shakespeare on William Butler Yeats may profit from a major advisor who is a specialist in modern Irish poetry and a second advisor who is a Shakespearean; a student working on a biophysics project could have both a biologist and a physicist as advisors; and a French major writing a play as a thesis project may wish to have faculty from both the theatre and French departments as advisors. This last example also suggests that students pursuing a thesis outside the normal range of projects in their major may nonetheless profit from the involvement of a faculty member in their major department who is familiar with their abilities and previous work.

A few honors programs and colleges require an "outside reader" or neutral advisor for thesis projects to ensure consistent standards for the thesis. Such a practice has potential advantages and disadvantages. This faculty member from a department outside the student's major could be the ideal catalyst for original thinking and work that does not get bogged down in conventional disciplinary practices and perspectives. Yet the lack of a disciplinary connection often makes an outside reader difficult to recruit for thesis work and sometimes limits the reader's commitment to it. Second, a reader outside the student's major or area of the thesis project may have no real understanding of the field or the topic, although some honors programs and colleges encourage their students to be able to explain their thesis work to someone outside their discipline. This demand may not be a problem with a history thesis or a business plan, which should be comprehensible to people with a variety of backgrounds, but it may become a serious concern in many other disciplines, particularly in the sciences and math.

The advantages of requiring only one advisor have made it the preferred model in most honors programs and colleges in the United States. Selecting a single thesis advisor not only fits the traditional model for thesis mentoring, but many honors directors and deans, whether at small liberal arts colleges with few faculty or at large research universities with an overwhelming number of thesis students, believe that it is the only option that would be practical at their institutions. For many, no viable alternatives exist. Because of demands on their faculty and the current constraints on financial and staff support for thesis work, one honors director declared: "It would be simply impossible for us to require more than one thesis advisor for the honors thesis."

INVOLVING ADVISORS IN THE THESIS PROPOSAL AND WORK PLAN

Most of the day-to-day responsibility for overseeing honors thesis work falls on the faculty member directly supervising a student's thesis project. As we noted earlier, honors directors should provide thesis advisors with information and suggestions that will direct their students towards successful thesis work. As they should with students, honors directors and deans must communicate early and often with thesis advisors, providing them with basic thesis information, an overview of the thesis process, including thesis requirements, timelines, and due dates. Providing thesis advisors with information about the current activities of honors thesis students and timely reminders of events and deadlines is also an effective way of keeping communication paths open to faculty advisors.

Faculty who are first-time thesis advisors may require special attention, but all faculty advisors can profit from discussing their duties and sharing advice on some issues they may face. One effective strategy for encouraging good thesis mentoring is scheduling a group meeting of thesis advisors early in the term. A working lunch usually attracts faculty. At such meetings, faculty are often most responsive when veteran thesis advisors can talk about their experiences, offer advice to new thesis advisors, and answer any questions that they might have.

The thesis advisor is the indispensable factor in developing a sound thesis proposal. Thesis advisors will know better than an honors director or dean whether a given topic is substantial enough for an advanced undergraduate to explore, manageable within a student's academic preparation and experience, and yet narrow enough to be completed by the student's anticipated graduation date. Of course, students are expected to develop their own thesis proposals, but the thesis advisor will always need to provide input and direction to assist in the process.

Honors thesis programs often make sample thesis proposals available to both faculty and students either as handouts or online, and students benefit when advisors review a few sample proposals with them. Such discussions of thesis proposals can clarify the parameters and expectations for a thesis project without intimidating the student, bringing thesis requirements down to realistic possibilities and ensuring that both the faculty advisor and thesis student share a common conception of the thesis. Most importantly, advisors should impress on their students that revising research plans and writing more than one draft of the research proposal are perfectly normal parts of professional research. Even though some students may see such revisions as painful setbacks, spending time refining the proposal is rarely wasted because a well-crafted proposal will give students the confidence and clear sense of direction they need for successful thesis work.

A thesis cannot be completed in a frenzy of activity at the end of a semester, nor will students benefit from a relationship with the thesis advisor without regular interactions. Some honors programs and colleges require thesis students to complete detailed work plans that function essentially as contracts protecting both faculty advisors and thesis students. Other honors programs and colleges leave such matters to the discretion of individual advisors. Nevertheless, most honors administrators agree that establishing some sort of timeline will keep thesis students on track and progressing in their work. The thesis student should not need constant handholding, but he or she should be meeting with the thesis advisor on a regular basis and completing something, however minimal, for each deadline.

Prudent thesis advisors will encourage students to build some additional time into their work plan to allow for the inevitable and unexpected problems that will arise, the research and writing blocks they will encounter, the times when creativity and insight are clouded and experiments go awry. When possible, the timeline should also take into account such things as visits to graduate and professional schools, internships, interviews, and the myriad other things that tug at students during the senior year. Honors thesis advisors should recognize that students often have many commitments that may not be obvious to faculty, such as campus organizations, work obligations, and athletics. Students' priorities sometimes vary widely from those of faculty, as indeed they should. Therefore, thesis advisors may need to prod their students gently about time management, commitment, and priorities that are appropriate for successful thesis work.

ADDRESSING THESIS EXPENSES AND POSSIBLE SOURCES OF FUNDING

Some thesis projects may require financial support. For example, some thesis work will require travel, substantial charges for photocopying, the purchase or rental of materials and equipment, and perhaps even the payment for use of campus space or facilities. Students in the sciences and the fine arts will often face substantial costs for supplies. The honors director or dean needs to let students and thesis advisors know of possible sources of funding, such as honors program or honors college research funds or special funds from alumni for honors thesis work.

Thesis advisors are in the best position to explain the likely costs of a thesis project to their students. In addition, they may be familiar with some of the ways such expenses might be defrayed. Faculty advisors are sometimes able to support thesis expenses from their own funds for research or professional activities, some departments have funding available for student researchers, and the college or university may have set aside funds to support undergraduate research. Because such funding sources often have early application deadlines, thesis advisors should prompt students to get thesis work, especially proposals, and funding applications underway as soon as possible.

In addition, honors administrators and faculty advisors should always encourage students to contact the chairs of their departments for possible assistance with their travel, conference registration, and other expenses. Sometimes a department head has funds or knows of other funding sources available to support student presentations. As noted earlier, departmental alumni are often eager to help aspiring students in their discipline. Honors administrators can even encourage students to contact higher levels of their institution's administration—a dean, the provost, or even the college or university president—because they always have some discretionary funds at their disposal.

Students working on their honors thesis usually receive a warm welcome from department chairs and other administrators, and it is surprising how often these personal requests for financial support are successful. Department chairs very much want to know about outstanding students in their departments, the projects they are working on, and the successful mentoring work by someone in their department. For a dean, provost, or president, a visit by a student usually comes as a welcome break from the academic pathology and budget problems that fill their days. They take pride in the accomplishments of honors thesis students, the institution's promotion of undergraduate research, and the institutional excellence represented by student conference presentations. No matter what the outcome, these administrators will not easily forget the student's visit, and they may lay the groundwork for future decisions regarding honors support, student research, and conference presentations.

ENCOURAGING STUDENTS TO PRESENT AND PUBLISH THEIR RESEARCH

Honors directors, deans, and thesis advisors should encourage students to present their thesis research and creativity locally, regionally, and nationally. For most students, conference proposals and presentations are new and sometimes intimidating events; both the thesis advisor and the honors director need to help students with their preparation. Students often value these presentations as much as they do their thesis work. Such presentations provide them with outside validation of their abilities. Student presentations and publications also highlight the quality of work done by faculty advisors and by their departments.

Local presentation of thesis work has many advantages, whether this happens in regular classes, special campus events, or institutional research days. Local presentations involve no travel or conference registration costs, and the low pressure associated with such events, especially when student peers are also making presentations and friends are in the audience, can make such presentations a less threatening experience for students. In honors programs and colleges that require a public presentation of thesis research, local research days are an especially good opportunity for thesis-related presentations, even if the thesis has not been completed. The organizers of these events do their best to include as many students as possible; consequently, their lead times for proposals are shorter. Also, the selection process is often less rigorous than it is for regional and national conferences or for refereed publications. And at some colleges or universities, experienced honors students have organized workshops on effective presentation strategies for other student presenters at the institution.

Faculty advisors can also encourage their students to submit papers and posters for regional and national disciplinary conferences, and honors administrators can supplement these opportunities with those offered by honors conferences. Every institution has a few faculty members who pride themselves on the number of presentations their students do, and these faculty can offer valuable assistance to advisors and students interested in doing such presentations. Prominent among these opportunities are the conferences and publications of the National Collegiate Honors Council (NCHC), national competitions for outstanding student research such as the NCHC's Portz Scholars Program, state and regional honors conferences, and the conferences and publications of the National Council for Undergraduate Research (NCUR).

Financial support for off-campus presentations is sometimes available if students look in the right places. The role of the honors administrator and thesis advisor in this search for financial support should be to motivate and guide a student's efforts, not to take over the funding search. Because securing funding is an integral part of professional work, this, too, may be a valuable learning experience for a thesis student. Many institutions have recently established programs to support undergraduate research, and some college benefactors have provided special funds for student research, travel, and presentation expenses.

In addition to conference presentations, there are a large number of options for the publication of student research. Honors directors, deans, and thesis advisors are indispensable in pointing students towards possible venues for publication and the types of articles they favor. Some honors programs and colleges publish journals that accept student submissions from across the country; national honors journals regularly include submissions from students; and still other journals are devoted entirely to undergraduate research, even if the student is not affiliated with an honors program or college. Moreover, if the thesis advisor thinks that the student's work is especially noteworthy, he or she may encourage the student to submit that work as an article to a professional journal in their discipline, perhaps jointly written with the faculty advisor. Some professional journals actively encourage student work and give it special consideration.

HELPING THESIS ADVISORS SOLVE PROBLEMS

As we have said repeatedly, thesis advisors deserve much credit for guiding their students through successful completion of the honors thesis. Yet despite all their efforts, problems will arise. Sometimes students become too stressed to do their work, or they procrastinate their way to failure. Experiments can fail. Interlibrary loans may not show up on time. Computers may die and files become lost or hopelessly corrupted. Funding may fall through. Students may fall seriously ill or become debilitated by an injury. In such circumstance, the thesis advisor and sometimes the honors director or dean need to be proactive by offering counsel and assistance to the student as soon as possible.

Honors directors and deans can help thesis advisors work through student problems in two ways. First, they can assure thesis advisors that they, the advisors, are trusted to make sound adjustments to their student's thesis project and that the honors director will back up the faculty member's professional judgment. Faculty usually know their student's thesis work best and certainly understand what adjustments can and should be made to the project to accommodate unforeseen circumstances. Second, honors directors and deans should make thesis advisors aware that they are always available to sort out student problems and resolve institutional difficulties. Sometimes, just listening to the concerns of thesis advisors is all that is necessary to assist them in solving problems. It is also important to remind thesis advisors that seniors completing the thesis are often under considerable stress. Graduate and professional school interviews, job searches, and life crises—such as anxiety about life after college!—can all interfere with thesis progress.

Several strategies exist to help students deal with these problems. One of the most effective is for thesis advisors to have their thesis students establish a schedule and urge them to stick to it. Most thesis students have never had to schedule a project of this magnitude into their daily academic and co-curricular lives, so it is important to help them set aside certain times each day or week to make progress. Sample timelines in thesis handbooks and on honors program websites are helpful for students and faculty alike, particularly faculty who are new to thesis advising.

Another effective strategy is requiring thesis students to submit regular, brief, written progress reports to the honors director, signed off on by the thesis advisor. Having these reports submitted to the honors director or dean ensures oversight and consistency throughout the thesis program. Providing a concrete record of students' progress will help them understand the need to budget their time and stay on track.

ASSESSING AND GRADING THE THESIS AND ITS PRESENTATION

In most cases the thesis advisor, who has the expertise to assess the student's work properly, evaluates and grades the honors thesis. A completed thesis usually holds no unpleasant surprises: the advisor has already seen early drafts, pointed out the rough patches, and suggested areas for improvement. The advisor is familiar with normal grading standards for work at the institution and usually has little trouble assigning an appropriate grade for the thesis. At many institutions, the thesis advisor is also asked to certify that the thesis meets the standards for an honors thesis and confirms this achievement by signing off on the thesis on a thesis approval form. In the case of a non-traditional thesis, based on, say, a performance, a film, or a marketing plan, grading the thesis will likely depend on the performance, film, or plan as well as on the written thesis.

Usually signing off on a thesis occurs without a hitch; however, thesis grading and approval sometimes become problematic when the student's thesis work is insufficient, of questionable quality, or perhaps clearly substandard. If the student is clearly responsible for the substandard work, the advisor may assign a lower grade for the thesis, perhaps even withholding approval of the thesis until the student makes any necessary revisions. When outside factors are at the root of poor or incomplete thesis work, some honors programs utilize additional options for grading, for approval, for number of credits awarded, and even for awarding the honors designation to the thesis. We should emphasize, however, that the appropriate course of action in these cases is highly dependent on the student's specific circumstances and the policies and philosophy of the individual honors program or college.

Of course, problems will occur, and they often raise serious issues for the faculty advisor and honors director or dean. For example, what is the appropriate course of action when a student has a severe illness or accident that clearly affects the quantity and quality of work done for the thesis? Should a poor or incomplete thesis block graduation for this student? Should the student be given an Incomplete and required to complete the thesis in a subsequent term despite commitments already made to graduate school or an employer? Could the student be given fewer credits for the thesis work? Can the honors thesis be reregistered as a conventional thesis? Or should an inadequate thesis simply be approved, the honors requirements satisfied, and the unsatisfactory performance indicated solely by a "B-" or lower for the course? We will explore these issues as well as other problems in Chapter 5.

In most cases, however, thesis work comes to a successful conclusion, and the thesis advisor grades and approves the thesis without a problem. After this stage, the thesis is usually forwarded to the honors college or program for the honors dean, director, or honors staff to review. This second level of approval is typically pro forma at most institutions because thesis advisors, with their acknowledged expertise in the area of the thesis project and their familiarity with the student's work, are in the best position to evaluate the completed thesis. While some honors directors read all of the theses completed in their program, most skim them only to make sure that they fulfill the particular honors requirements.

A few honors programs and colleges require an oral defense of the undergraduate honors thesis. Such defenses may be formal presentations, involving questions by faculty and students; more often they are more relaxed discussions of the thesis work with a few faculty members. Some honors programs require a public presentation rather than a defense. Thesis students are often allowed to select the venue for this presentation, including in other classes at the institution (perhaps a class taught by the thesis advisor); presentations at local, regional, or national conferences; or to community groups likely to be interested in their work. Such required presentations are normally not graded. Because some thesis students have anxieties about these presentations and have little relevant experience to call on, an honors program that requires public defense or presentation of theses should offer students appropriate practice sessions or training workshops.

Despite their anxieties, thesis students usually do not resist doing oral presentations. They know their material and are happy to share it. The presentation brings them a real sense of pride and closure. Discussing their thesis work in a public forum gives students a profound feeling of accomplishment beyond that of having completed a heavy written thesis: a feeling of having something to contribute. By presenting research work and ideas that they have created and made their own, they are validating their role as scholars.

ESTABLISHING AND MAINTAINING A THESIS LIBRARY

A thesis library is not just a storage place for completed theses; it is a manifestation of the institutional recognition of the value and quality of honors thesis work. Honors theses exemplify the best and most advanced undergraduate work at the institution, and like master's theses and doctoral dissertations, they should be accessible to the public and to other students. A thesis library or archive is an excellent resource for students searching for their own thesis topics and considering the amount and quality of work that a thesis will entail. Many students commit to doing a thesis only after reading several previous theses and recognizing that a thesis project is within their abilities. For this reason many honors programs and colleges require students to read earlier theses, often in their thesis preparation courses.

Some programs have established a thesis archive within the college or university library; others house it in the honors facility, and some departments house honors theses in their own office or lounge. While many honors programs and colleges still retain hard copies of honors theses, colleges and universities are increasingly relying on digital media to archive theses. This step makes it easy for students, thesis advisors, and the general public to access completed theses 24/7 from anywhere in the world with a computer or even a smart phone.

A "heads up" for honors directors and deans is necessary at this point. Just as contemporary marketing schemes offer honors students meaningless memberships in dubious "honor societies," making a good profit from membership fees or by selling copies of a book containing the student's listing, similar ploys are now targeting students who have completed an honors thesis. One international "publishing" company, operating under a variety of imprints and listing offices in Germany, Latvia, Moldova, and Mauritius, claims to be digitizing more than 50,000 dissertations and theses a month, downloading them from institutional websites. These companies offer authors a "free" printed copy of the thesis *if they agree to sign away their rights to the thesis.* The companies make their profit by charging more than $60 for each additional copy of the thesis bought for family and friends. As Joseph Stromberg points out in "I Sold my Undergraduate Thesis to a Print Content Farm" (2014), students are being offered print-on-demand services no better than those available at the local copy shop, where two or three similar copies of a thesis can be printed and bound for less than $20. *Caveat emptor.*

Archiving completed theses should not be considered simply a formality or mechanical task, like placing athletic awards in a trophy case. Archiving undergraduate honors theses, like master's theses and doctoral dissertations, testifies to their value at the institution and to others outside it. A thesis library or archive of completed honors theses also plays a significant role in the way that the thesis is perceived by students working on their project. Because honors theses are archived after completion, students have clear evidence that this research is considered more significant than class activities or research papers completed in normal courses: finished then easily forgotten or thrown away. Knowing that all honors theses are archived, students recognize that their own thesis is likely to be available well beyond their Facebook postings or Instagram pictures. To put it simply, because their honors thesis will be easily available to their fellow students, to faculty, and to the general public, students need to take thesis work seriously. Just as cover letters display a student's writing abilities, an honors thesis provides valuable evidence about a student's academic preparation, intellectual abilities, capacity for effectively organizing work, and willingness to take on independent tasks. Potential employers can look over a student's honors thesis just as easily as they now examine his or her Facebook pages.

The existence of a thesis library also has a positive impact on faculty thesis advisors and their commitment to helping students do the best possible work. Because the faculty advisor's name appears on the finished thesis, the thesis reflects the faculty member's judgment and mentoring abilities as well as the student's work. Faculty advisors know that they too will be judged on the quality of the thesis their student produces, and they have strong motivation to ensure that any thesis they direct and approve reflects well on them, especially in the eyes of their departmental colleagues. Consequently, they are likely to maintain high standards that are consistent with those of other faculty and to work hard to bring their thesis students up to this level.

Honors directors and deans usually take honors approval of a thesis seriously because it reflects the standards, consistency, and even the fairness of their honors program or college. A few cases of inadequate thesis work can tarnish the perception of and the quality of both honors work and undergraduate work in general at the institution. It confuses students about what will be expected of them, exposes inconsistencies in faculty standards, and implies poor management and oversight in the honors program. In the early stages of thesis work, students and faculty advisors frequently look at previous theses, and students quickly pick up on inconsistent standards and the acceptance of inadequate work by others. "Why should I have to write a 50-page thesis when three years ago Terry had a 15-page thesis accepted?" "Why should I have to do so much rewriting when Joe didn't even proofread his thesis?" "Why do I have to include so much documentation when Stacy got away with just six references—and two of them were from Wikipedia?!" Obviously, the best way to avoid these problems is to make sure that all theses meet honors program standards.

Thus, a thesis library reinforces the importance of maintaining quality in thesis work. The archiving of theses provides an honors program or college with a compelling rationale for insisting that every thesis must meet minimum standards of quality and must fulfill other honors requirements, including reflective statements, common thesis format, and appropriate documentation. Honors theses need to maintain high standards because students are presenting these theses as examples of their independent academic achievement, approved by a faculty advisor and the honors program, and implicitly reflecting the best undergraduate work at the institution. At most colleges and universities, the honors director or dean is the person ultimately responsible for ensuring that all theses meet honors standards. In effect, honors program approval of the thesis confers an institutional imprimatur on the thesis, and the public archiving of honors theses reflects this process and illustrates the honors status of the thesis.

CELEBRATING STUDENT SUCCESS AND RECOGNIZING FACULTY CONTRIBUTIONS

Honors directors and deans should celebrate the success of those students who complete the thesis and program, just as colleges and universities celebrate students' completion of their undergraduate work with a graduation ceremony. For honors programs or colleges that take pride in their small group interactions and close working relationships between faculty and students, special honors recognition ceremonies seem most appropriate. Students will see some of their peers and their professors for the last time before graduating, and they can celebrate the honors experience they have shared before moving on. Such honors program or college ceremonies provide a desirable closure to the academic year, to the rigors of thesis work, to the special achievements of students and faculty, and to a student's total undergraduate career and experience in honors.

At these honors graduation ceremonies, many honors programs and colleges award certificates or medals and provide a reception for family, friends, and colleagues. At a time when college graduation ceremonies are becoming increasingly crowded and impersonal, an intimate honors ceremony can be meaningful to students and their families. This event is an opportunity for the honors program or college to recognize notable student achievements and for faculty and family to participate in the celebration of student success. Family members can meet the thesis advisor, the honors dean or director, and other students in the honors college or program. The ceremony provides recognition and closure for everyone involved.

In addition to the celebration, some honors programs and colleges publish descriptions of honors theses completed during the year; these booklets also identify the thesis advisors, profile graduating thesis students, and mention the academic and professional plans these students have. Because the academic world commonly measures excellence by such accomplishments and awards, making the upper administration aware of its students' success is extremely important for an honors program or college. Inviting administrators to thesis presentations or ceremonies as well as sending them a copy of any compilation about thesis work is also wise. Of course, publicizing honors students' thesis work also highlights the quality of departmental teaching, research, and mentoring.

Such information about honors thesis students plays an increasingly important role in an institution's discussion of educational quality. Profiles of outstanding students and comments from students of diverse backgrounds about their undergraduate experiences may be of great interest to those off campus. Honors administrators have recognized that providing this information to admissions staff for student recruitment; to faculty and staff who address alumni groups; and to deans, vice-presidents, and presidents, who discuss academic excellence at their institution in a wide range of venues, can highlight the importance of the honors program or college and can lay a strong base for support from both the faculty and the administration.

The hard work and valuable contributions of faculty advisors are too often overlooked in contemporary colleges and universities. Honors directors and deans are uniquely positioned to recognize the high quality work done by faculty thesis advisors, and some honors directors have effectively lobbied for increasing the rewards at their institutions for faculty directing an undergraduate thesis. Some institutions provide thesis advisors with stipends for each honors thesis they advise or give faculty release/reassigned time credit for this work. For example, a department might give a faculty member who has advised a specific number of undergraduate theses and independent research projects the equivalent of one full course release or reassigned time. Some honors programs and colleges present thesis advisors with a modest honorarium, a gift certificate to the college bookstore, or a small gift to indicate that their work is much appreciated. And faculty will always welcome a letter for their personnel file that details the success of their work in mentoring thesis students.

Faculty also appreciate some public recognition. Again, the work of faculty advisors can be highlighted at the year-end honors ceremonies. The honors director or dean can ask advisors to stand and be recognized. Thesis advisors can take the stage to present their students with a graduation medal or certificate. If such ceremonies encourage students to say a few words about their thesis and their plans for the future, this speech is also a great opportunity for them to publicly thank their advisors. A photograph of student and advisor taken at this event might be sent to the faculty member's department, perhaps for publication in the department newsletter, posting on a bulletin board, or uploading to the department website. Such visible recognition of their thesis work can be even more meaningful to faculty than small stipends.

CHAPTER 4

The Thesis Preparation Course

In an ideal world, all honors students would be prepared to embark on an honors thesis with little or no assistance from the honors program or college. Indeed some are. They have taken all the appropriate courses and excelled in them. They were engaged by an idea or a topic early on, have taken an advanced course or two in pursuit of their topic, and are eager to explore some aspects of this topic further and in more depth. They have connected with and impressed professors who have shown an interest in them and their ideas and have a realistic grasp of their abilities. They may even have worked closely with the professor in the field, the lab, or the studio, and they are familiar with research practices in their discipline.

These students have the fundamental skills they will need in their thesis work. They write well, are familiar with standard documentation practices in their disciplines, and are prepared for the time commitment and intellectual demands that an honors thesis will require. They understand not only the importance of meeting regularly with their thesis advisor, but also that rethinking and rewriting are a normal and essential part of the intellectual process.

These students will likely submit their honors thesis on time, well written, original, thoughtful, and fully documented.

The decision to do an honors thesis seems almost a natural progression for the student who has been passionate about rocks since middle school, who caught the eye of a science teacher who hooked her up with a geology professor at the local college who took her on digs, and who comes into the honors program laser-focused on her passion. Or the student who first spent a year in France with his family, became fascinated by French literature, returned to France several times as an exchange student, and has decided to translate an underappreciated French poet into English. Students with this much passion and ability will, with luck and persistence, attract the attention of faculty members who will nurture their interests; inform them about valuable foreign study programs, internships, or research projects; and guide them into early planning for their honors thesis.

But for most students, the journey through college is not so smooth. Too often promising students never find the right path, struggle with a choice of major, fail to make a timely selection of a thesis topics or advisor, procrastinate in their research and writing, or lack the drive and commitment to complete a thesis. At one point or another, they give up on the thesis, sometimes even before they enroll in thesis courses because they look like too much work. Sometimes they come to a dead end after they have registered for the thesis course, prompting frantic late-term attempts to withdraw from the course or a fatalistic acceptance of a poor or failing grade for the thesis.

Even those students who want to write a thesis have problems. They may have trouble selecting a topic or choosing an advisor. Some are less knowledgeable in their fields because they did not settle on a major until their junior year. Some students delay starting their thesis while they consider other options, such as an internship, foreign study, or an additional major or minor. These students do want to write an honors thesis, but the path towards a successful project is more difficult for them to find.

While no honors director wants to see students fail, some failures are to be expected. Early promise does not guarantee success in college or in life. Despite the best efforts of directors to help students make good academic choices and succeed, they cannot save students from themselves. As most honors directors know, some honors students coasted through high school and can coast through their first years of college despite lacking the maturity to plan and follow through on an independent thesis project. Others just run out of steam, concluding that the reward-to-work ratio for the thesis makes it unattractive, preferring a less stressful senior year, or they find little value in doing an honors thesis when their plan is to work right after college. A significant number of honors students prefer to spend their senior year doing an internship, a community service project, a foreign study program, or another major or minor rather than an honors thesis. Directors should understand that these scenarios are fairly typical and will recur with some regularity.

THE RESPONSIBILITY OF THE HONORS PROGRAM FOR THESIS SUCCESSES

But when too many students fail to complete or even start a required thesis, the honors program or perhaps the larger institution may also bear some responsibility. The following personal experiences may be instructive. One of the authors inherited an honors program from an honors director whose philosophy was that honors program students should sink or swim on their own, that completing a thesis was a responsibility that students should be mature enough to handle themselves. "This is an honors program; these are incredibly smart and capable students; they've been given an excellent education in their majors, so they don't need any help on their theses from the honors program. It's all up to the students and their thesis advisor." The result of this philosophy of non-involvement was that, although the program admitted 75 students annually, only five or six completed a thesis each year, a success rate of 8% at best. What college would tolerate such a retention rate today? If an institution views its honors program simply as a marketing tool to attract superior freshmen, but then abandons them, it does a great disservice to the students, to the program, and to the institution. Neither the institution nor the students are getting what they should from honors. Unfortunately, such stories were not uncommon a few decades ago: another of the authors took over an honors program where the thesis completion rate was only 15–20%.

Such miserable thesis completion rates in these two honors programs were significantly improved in just a few years by some basic reforms. Rather than abandoning students after they had finished their lower-division honors courses, the honors directors recognized the need to do much more to encourage and support thesis work. As a first step, increased contacts were forged with juniors and seniors through group activities and advisement sessions. More significantly, both honors programs were redesigned to encourage steady progression towards thesis work, including adding required thesis preparation courses for juniors, instituting early deadlines for registering thesis projects and selecting faculty thesis advisors, and incorporating effective checkpoints and support programs for both thesis students and faculty advisors. As a consequence, within two or three years the vast majority of honors students at both institutions were completing an honors thesis; furthermore, their faculty advisors became strong advocates for the thesis mentoring experience and for honors work in general.

Although a few academics still cling to the idea that high failure rates suggest high standards, the idea that honors study should be an exercise in social Darwinism is no longer an acceptable educational paradigm. Colleges and universities today would not tolerate such low rates of student success in an honors program or elsewhere in the classes, departments, and programs at the institution. Honors programs and colleges across the country now focus on student-learning outcomes, intellectual development throughout an undergraduate's career, undergraduate research and professional opportunities, and the significant achievements of graduating students. While some institutions do use honors programs as a marketing tool to attract superior freshmen, institutions today are even more eager to demonstrate that their students are getting their money's worth from honors. In fact, at many institutions honors thesis students have come to represent superior achievement at the college or university.

Retention rates, of course, are context bound. American institutions have highly diverse educational roles and student bodies that will affect thesis work. An institution that attracts a significant number of transfer students, non-liberal-arts majors, or mature students or an honors program at an institution that heavily promotes student teaching, internships, and work-study opportunities may have very different retention rates and thesis completion rates than a traditional liberal arts institution that funnels a great many of its honors students into graduate study.

The honors community generally agrees that the primary responsibility for overseeing honors theses lies with faculty advisors and individual departments. Many thesis advisors indeed do a fine job without much honors assistance. Consequently, many honors directors and deans are reluctant to insert themselves into the thesis process, believing that whatever they might do could be seen as interference in what is essentially a faculty-student relationship and discipline-centered process.

But it is a mistake for honors directors and deans to believe that thesis completion rates or thesis quality will not benefit from their input and support. Thesis students frequently encounter situations where honors assistance can be extremely helpful. As noted earlier, recruiting a thesis advisor on their own is often difficult for students. Students proposing unusual or multidisciplinary topics or hoping to include non-traditional learning experiences into their thesis research may need assistance from the honors director or staff, perhaps even to the point of having them contact faculty and lobbying for a specific thesis project on behalf of the student. When a student encounters difficulties in finding an advisor to take on a thesis project, honors directors and their staff can often suggest other choices or recommend some adjustment to the student's thesis project.

DEPARTMENTAL EFFORTS TO IMPROVE THESIS PREPARATION

Departmental requirements and research opportunities can also help to prepare students for advanced research and an honors thesis. Some departments require all their majors to take research methods courses. These courses typically discuss various methodologies and their pros and cons; they may even have students doing some research. They do not, however, usually teach students about how to select a research topic in the real world or how to massage that topic into a viable research project. They do not teach about time management or scarce resources. They do not discuss the seemingly endless writing and rewriting in preparing a thesis or the writer's block and the frustrations that thesis students may also encounter.

To deal with these sorts of issues, some departments at larger institutions have gone beyond conventional research methods courses to offer their own thesis preparation courses for honors students in their junior or senior years. These departments have a clear idea of what even their superior students need to prepare for advanced research, and they especially emphasize that, in order for a thesis to succeed at the highest level, thesis students and their faculty mentors must start the thesis process early. Hence, departmental thesis preparation courses are prerequisites to writing the thesis and focus on early tasks, such as how to write a thesis proposal, how to secure a thesis advisor, and how to find and utilize appropriate campus resources. They often delve deeper into research methodologies by working with primary sources and data analysis, and they usually include advice about time management, writing, and editing. Such courses also help students understand that honors thesis projects need focused approaches and early initiation in order to meet disciplinary standards for superior work.

From the perspective of an honors program or college, there are definite advantages when departments offer their own thesis preparation courses. First, these departmental classes ease the strain on the honors program or college because it does not have to use its resources to provide a one-size-fits-all course for a variety of majors. Second, this structure provides an opportunity for students to begin working closely with potential advisors in their majors. As noted above, who better to guide honors research than a faculty member in the student's discipline? Third, the classes allow students to bond and work with other students in the same field, perhaps in support groups. Finally, upper-division students are sometimes reluctant to take what they see as an extra honors course or requirement, but they are often willing to accept a similar course and requirement in their major discipline.

THE VALUE OF AN HONORS THESIS PREPARATION COURSE

Despite the effectiveness of junior- and senior-year departmental thesis prep courses, faculty often report that they very much appreciate honors involvement, not only in preparing students for thesis work but also in continuing support through the final stages of thesis work. Advisors see such involvement as an indication that the honors program recognizes their hard work and that of their thesis students and that the honors staff will provide assistance wherever and whenever it is needed. Thesis advisors count on the honors program to send them focused students who have some insight into the best practices for thesis work and who come to them early enough to establish productive mentoring relationships. Furthermore, honors involvement demonstrates that the institution as a whole is committed to making the work of both faculty advisor and thesis student as successful as possible.

Honors involvement is especially effective in preparing students for the realities of thesis work and the student's role in making the mentoring relationship work well. Students learn that at this stage of their academic career, they are expected to act professionally and be well prepared. Before they approach a potential advisor about a thesis project, they need to have given some thought to what it will entail, even if they have not worked the project out in detail. This preparedness and professionalism are also important for future meetings with their thesis advisor. If students are unprepared, mentoring meetings are likely to be unproductive, a waste of both the student's and advisor's time. In such cases, the advisor may feel obligated to tell the student exactly what to do rather than working out issues together. Unproductive or dictatorial meetings with a faculty advisor can also be discouraging for students; hence, they may disappear after a meeting or two and give up on the thesis.

Even worse, from the faculty advisor's point of view, are the students who have the misconception that they can be completely independent in their thesis work. After an initial meeting or two with the advisor, the student disappears for months, only to show up a few days before graduation with a "finished" manuscript in hand—unadvised, unedited, and often unacceptable. At this point, there is often little that the faculty advisor can do except call the honors office to alert them about this situation. The experience of such thesis failures has become a strong incentive for many honors deans and directors to improve their thesis programs in ways that would minimize such disasters.

With few exceptions, even the smartest and most capable students can benefit from a thesis preparation course as the starting point in their thesis work. While students may have a strong interest in a topic, the passion to pursue it in some new direction, and the necessary preparation in their discipline, they sometimes lack the organizational strategies to get a thesis off the ground and bring it to a timely completion. If they are lucky, students may receive solid research and writing strategies from courses or support activities in their department. Because many small departments are unable to offer departmental research methods courses or a special thesis preparation course, it may fall to the honors program to offer a thesis preparation course that supplies honors students with the structure for thesis work and communicates effective strategies for its successful completion.

While every honors thesis is unique, most honors directors feel that all theses share enough common elements to make an honors thesis preparation course viable and effective. At many institutions an honors prep course is a practical way of communicating to students the special requirements and standards for an honors thesis: the expectations, qualities, and components that distinguish it from a non-honors research projects. Moreover, every thesis experience is also subject to a common set of potential problems, problems that an honors thesis preparation course can deal with effectively in a systematic way. In addition, an honors thesis preparation course sends a clear message to students, faculty, and administrators: the honors thesis is the final and perhaps most important element in an honors program. For honors students it is an advanced-level project that is the culmination of an undergraduate's academic career.

The following description of a thesis preparation course clarifies both the objectives and the typical content for such a course.

> [The thesis preparation course] has two purposes: (1) to help students create a quality honors thesis, and (2) to help students complete this thesis on time . . . [and] before their scheduled graduation. To this end, students in this seminar will select a thesis topic, choose their thesis advisors, and develop a thesis proposal with their advisors—including a statement of the thesis topic, a hypothesis (where appropriate), a description of the major tasks the student and advisor feel are needed to complete the thesis, a review of the resources the thesis will draw upon, a bibliography, and a timetable for the thesis project. In other words, students in [this course] actively begin serious work on their honors thesis. To help students with these tasks, they meet regularly with other honors students who are working on their thesis projects and with the Honors Program staff to discuss thesis requirements, mutual problems, and possible solutions. (SUNY Oswego)

A thesis prep course can teach students, regardless of discipline, essentials necessary to carry through a project both in the academic world and beyond, skills they may not have learned in a discipline-based research methods course. It can help them understand deadlines, scheduling, collegiality, and consultation. Even more importantly, students can move beyond just learning about research methods into the real-world task of constructing and refining a solid research proposal, developing an effective work plan with clear indications of progress and deadlines, and revising early drafts of the thesis into a compelling product that meets the standards for inclusion in the college library, online distribution, and possible oral presentation.

Although faculty know that writing means revising, rewriting, and producing multiple drafts before the finished project is reached, most undergraduate coursework does little to prepare students for the inevitable give-and-take of the thesis process. Students often assume that whatever they hand in, either as a proposal or as the thesis, is essentially the final product, perhaps needing a few minor emendations. They are often taken aback when their thesis advisor tells them that what they have written is a good start and useful first draft, but that they need to make some revisions before it can be approved. To the extent that an honors thesis prep course can address not just thesis requirements but also the realities of thesis work, it makes the mentoring relationship between faculty and student much more collegial as well as more productive.

The primary value of a thesis preparation course is to guide students into an early start on their thesis projects. In a typical prep course, students must refine their initial ideas for a thesis project into a short list of possible topics, meet with potential thesis advisors, assemble an initial bibliography, and evaluate important sources. The thesis preparation course also maintains the honors community established in lower-division courses and adapts it to support advanced projects and individualized topics. Honors students tend to be busy students, and many honors directors have found that, without a thesis prep course to demonstrate to students that an honors thesis is a worthwhile and doable pursuit, even the best-intentioned students may drift away from this capstone experience. Simply put, a thesis prep course provides external stimulus and support for successful thesis work.

A thesis prep course offers a perfect opportunity to reemphasize to students the importance of reliable sources, sound argumentation, and appropriate documentation, whatever the discipline. The course can also reacquaint students with the various resources in the library and elsewhere at the institution that will support their research. Instructors in such prep courses are often surprised by the holes in their upper-division students' knowledge of even the most basic of these resources.

Moreover, students have been trained through the years to think and plan in one-semester chunks, often throwing together a research paper for a course in a few weeks at the end of the semester. A junior-year thesis prep course helps students to understand that a thesis will require much more planning and forethought, as well as a higher degree of problem solving and perhaps even creativity in comparison to their previous work. Finally, this course can effectively impress upon students that *they* bear significant responsibility for successful meetings with their thesis advisor, that *they* must set many of the interim deadlines for their research and writing, and that *they* must solve problems or adjust their thesis work as warranted. For honors students this course becomes the starting point for an advanced-level project that will be the culmination of their undergraduate careers.

Many honors directors and deans believe that the thesis preparation course has a greater impact on thesis success and completion rates than any other aspect of their thesis programs. Their experience demonstrates that the vast majority of honors students can complete a thesis if they receive the timely support they need, both from honors staff and from their fellow students. The benefits for individual students are obvious, especially at institutions where the thesis is a requirement for honors graduation, but thesis advisors, departments, and the honors program or college also benefit: better-prepared students produce a higher-quality thesis and graduate with honors at a higher rate. This accomplishment is a laudable one for the honors program or college, the student's major department, and the institution as a whole.

STAFFING AND SCHEDULING A THESIS PREPARATION COURSE

At many institutions the thesis preparation course is taught by the honors director or dean or by other honors staff familiar with undergraduate research and the program's thesis requirements. Sometimes additional faculty or college support staff may also be brought into the course, perhaps a research librarian or a member of the institution's writing center. A thesis prep course is often where students receive a thesis handbook or handouts on specific thesis-related topics. A number of thesis prep courses require students to read several completed theses in their area. This hands-on examination of other honors theses is one of the most productive aspects of a thesis preparation course. It gives students a realistic idea of what is possible, what is acceptable, what they need to do or should not do. Reading earlier theses helps students understand what a thesis actually involves and motivates them in their thesis work: "If this is what a thesis is, I can do it, and I am ready to start right now."

Honors directors who have inadequately funded and understaffed programs may well see a required thesis preparation course as a further strain on their resources. Why not simply give students a series of handouts discussing the thesis? Or why not offer an optional thesis prep course just for those students who want to take it? While these steps are better than no preparation, a required thesis prep course has some advantages. Most obviously, a mandatory thesis preparation course requires students to prepare for their thesis work. It overcomes hesitations, gets students started on their own projects, and guides them through the thesis process in a systematic and coherent way.

Beyond this assistance, a thesis prep course brings students together in a supportive environment. With the honors thesis process looming ahead, some students develop feelings of inferiority and believe that other honors students are better prepared than they are. They often believe that the thesis is beyond them, that they have neither the time nor the ability to do successful thesis work. Yet when brought together with some of their classmates in a thesis prep course, they learn that they are not the only ones having trouble picking a topic or an advisor and not the only ones having trouble getting motivated, scheduling meetings and deadlines, or writing. This experience can be eye-opening, even liberating. In a required thesis prep course, students can share their problems and their solutions as they move forward on their individual thesis projects.

Our review of honors thesis programs found that such preparatory courses typically are required for all honors students in their junior year. An honors thesis prep course begun in the junior year forces students to take important steps early on in the process: they think about their topic, select a thesis advisor and topic from a number of possibilities, and even situate their thesis work in the context of the other courses and activities they want to pursue in their senior year. Even with tight junior year schedules and often inflexible course requirements in their majors, most students are able to fit this honors course into their schedules, particularly if it can be a one- or two-credit-hour course offered at different times. For those who cannot take it during the junior year, perhaps because of studying abroad or internships, the thesis preparation course can be taken in the summer or during the first term of the senior year.

Some honors programs that start the thesis in the junior year also offer senior year meetings, online discussions, or even seminars for students in the midst of their thesis work to maintain student involvement and interaction. Senior year often presents new challenges for honors students working on a thesis, challenges that students may not feel comfortable discussing with the honors director or their thesis advisor. Thesis students often encounter down periods when they lack motivation, feel overwhelmed by graduation demands, or have flagging confidence or flagging interest in thesis work. Sharing problems and solutions with other students in the same situation can help them address these issues more easily and more honestly than talking with a faculty advisor.

Most thesis preparation courses are 1-to-3-credit courses. The 3-credit thesis prep course obviously covers the most ground, discussing the differences in disciplinary research practices, examining variations of the thesis, and exploring possible thesis topics or areas that students may not have considered. In many cases the 3-credit thesis prep course has students begin the actual research, writing, and documentation of their thesis. Starting first drafts of the thesis is particularly valuable, even if a student later modifies or changes the thesis topic, because such work sets the thesis in motion and proves to students that they have the ability to do sound thesis research and writing. After completion of the thesis preparation course, students just need to continue on the trajectory they have established while working with their advisor to make adjustments as necessary.

Despite the obvious value of a 3-credit thesis prep course, offering one can be problematic. Teaching a 3-credit thesis prep course often lays another burden on the honors directors or honors staff members who typically teach this course. Finding regular faculty willing to give up one of their disciplinary courses in order to teach this course can be difficult. Fitting another upper-division 3-credit course into their schedules may be equally difficult for the students. The thesis prep course may conflict with required courses in students' majors: experienced honors directors and deans know that no matter when a prep course is offered, a few students will be unable to work it into their schedules. Finally, although the thesis prep course is intended to ease students into the thesis, students may see another 3-credit course as burdensome and intimidating.

Because of the difficulties in staffing and scheduling a 3-credit thesis preparation course, many honors directors have opted to offer a more basic 1-credit thesis prep course. If a thesis preparation course is important, then it is equally important to ensure that students can actually take the course without compromising their work in their major, their other academic options, and their other commitments and activities. To this end, programs that offer a 1-credit thesis prep course that meets for one hour a week usually offer several sections on different days to accommodate student schedules. Students see the 1-credit course as easier to fit into their schedules and less time consuming, an acceptable option while they mull over whether or not to do an honors thesis.

Clearly, a 1-credit thesis preparation course cannot cover as much material as a 3-credit course. Still, for many honors programs, a 1-credit thesis prep course is both a practical and effective option at their institutions. Despite the fact that the course may meet in a classroom for only an hour each week or be taught partially or totally online, most of the objectives of a more extensive thesis preparation course can still be covered: selecting a topic, finding an advisor, exploring the library, looking for sources, and preparing a proposal. The class meetings, whether online or in a classroom, can be largely devoted to reviewing and clarifying thesis requirements and strategies; making assignments that will enable students to get a sound start on their individual projects; and providing a forum where students can discuss their concerns, the problems they are encountering, and the solutions they have found.

On the other hand, it must be admitted that offering a required thesis preparation course just for honors program students, even when the course is only a 1-credit requirement, can create some difficulties. Staffing and scheduling a required junior/senior course may be a challenge. At small institutions or in new honors programs, the number of thesis students may not justify a stand-alone thesis preparation course. Furthermore, in large honors programs or colleges where there are scores, perhaps even hundreds, of honors students doing a thesis every year, scheduling, staffing, and financing many sections of a thesis preparation course may simply make a required thesis preparation course unfeasible.

OTHER OPTIONS FOR THESIS PREPARATION COURSES

The difficult situations outlined above may provide the motivation to create new formats for a thesis preparation course. Because honors students are already experienced learners who are expected to design an original thesis project on which they will work independently, a prep course that does not require fixed class meetings every week can also be successful. Some thesis prep courses start with regular meetings of the entire class, but have fewer meetings as the term progresses and the students are working more intently on the preparations for their own thesis project. Other courses may begin with a few meetings of the entire class, then break down into smaller groups that meet at more convenient times. A faculty member's presence is not always necessary for this small-group work, especially if group reports and assignments provide the instructor with some oversight. If student groups wish to meet in a coffee shop at 8:00 a.m. or in a residence hall for pizza at 11:00 p.m., that is their decision.

Guest faculty and staff can be a great source for instructional assistance in a thesis preparation course, and their meetings with students can be a valuable substitute for regular course meetings. Reference librarians love working with honors students, and they can usually schedule group meetings to address the use of inter-library loan services, to outline special library collections and facilities, to discuss important online bibliographies and resources, to explain any special checkout policies that the library may have for honors thesis students, and to arrange for the book lockers and study carrels. Staff at the college's writing center are equally happy to meet with groups of honors students to discuss the best strategies for large research and writing projects, the different formats that are appropriate for theses in various disciplines, and the standard bibliographic formats used in such disciplines. An added benefit of having these expert faculty and staff involved in the thesis prep course is that thesis students are much more comfortable approaching them for individual assistance later in their thesis work.

Sometimes a faculty member teaching a conventional research methods course will agree to take on a group of students preparing to start their thesis work, offering them a few extra sessions specifically directed at honors thesis work. Other faculty members in various disciplines might be persuaded to hold one or two hour-long round table discussions on thesis work in their areas. They may even want to bring in a professional or a graduate student in the field to provide additional perspectives for the students. Support from the honors director or dean is often a crucial element in making such teaching arrangements possible, even when offering financial compensation to the faculty member is not possible.

Using other, more-advanced thesis students as instructional staff in a thesis preparation course is invaluable. Honors directors and deans who are familiar with peer mentoring and tutorial programs for entering freshmen in honors already understand the impact such programs can have and how easily such programs can be adapted for thesis students. Whether the mentors are students who just recently completed an honors thesis or those still in the process of completing a thesis, their testimony and experiences hit home with students who are just starting thesis work. Students who are starting a thesis in the sciences are likely to find an informal talk with a student completing an honors thesis in chemistry more valuable than the general wisdom and good advice given them by faculty with a PhD in literature or sociology.

Peer instruction can be effective in a variety of formats. Students can take over the instruction for a class or two to discuss specific aspects of thesis work, from research problems and effective writing strategies to work plans, time management, and meetings with a faculty advisor. When talking to their peers, students are often astonishingly candid about their own experiences and insightful about what other students should and should not do during the thesis process. Honors directors can bring experienced thesis students into a thesis prep class, or they could meet individually with disciplinary groups without faculty supervision. Frequently these students will be happy to meet with other students several times or be on-call for them if they have any problems.

Two other suggestions may prove valuable. First, if the honors program is not in a position to offer a thesis prep course, honors administrators might encourage individual departments to offer or strengthen their own thesis prep courses and/or offer informal small group meetings or seminars for honors thesis students. Second, even under difficult circumstances, an honors program or college still has some obligation to prepare and support its students in their thesis effort. If a thesis preparation course is not possible, programs should at least prepare and distribute a comprehensive series of handouts related to thesis work or aggregate them into a thesis handbook that can be easily distributed to students and faculty advisors. Such handouts would include a clear statement of thesis requirements, the forms and processes that need to be completed, required sections and formats for the thesis, and specific deadlines for the completion of various aspects of thesis work. All of these materials should be available online as well for easy reference by students and faculty. Some steps may replicate activities sponsored by departments, but, when it comes to supporting students with the honors thesis, more is better.

PUTTING A THESIS PREPARATION COURSE PARTIALLY OR COMPLETELY ONLINE

With current developments in digital technology and online instruction, a number of additional options might be useful in a thesis preparation course. Some honors programs and colleges already use online course management software such as Blackboard, Moodle, Canvas, and Angel in their honors courses. Others have special thesis forums or discussion groups on their websites or have adopted social media such as Facebook to supplement honors courses and activities.

Although some in honors may feel that the use of social media lacks the vital interactions that only a small seminar can provide, educators must remember that students are much more comfortable than faculty with digital media. Students used the college or university website when they applied for admission, they do their banking and shopping online, and the majority of college and university students sign in to Facebook on a daily basis. They use text messages to keep in contact with their friends and use a smart phone app to order pizza. Students not only turn to YouTube to explore the world and be entertained, but they probably have done extensive online work for some of their courses. Not surprisingly students often prefer to read previous honors theses online rather than in hard copy in the library. For many students, the convenience of online communication outweighs its limitations.

Putting an honors preparation course partially or entirely online can alleviate some of the problems with staffing and scheduling that often crop up whenever the course is offered. The size of an online class is not limited by the constraints of a classroom or the optimum number of students for good class discussions, and a single instructor can often handle a large number of students while still encouraging student contributions and interactions in the class. Most importantly, online instruction is accessible whenever the students have the time and wherever they might be located. Are they ever without their cell phones or access to the Internet? Even the student with a job or family responsibilities, the student in an overseas study program, or the student doing an out-of-town internship can participate fully in online assignments and discussions.

One of the authors began putting parts of a thesis preparation course online more than a decade ago and found that the online format can be used effectively for many of the assignments and activities typically featured in a classroom course. Naturally, adjustments need to be made to accommodate the realities of digital education. For example, an education professor once stated that the Internet forced her to change many aspects of her courses. She previously had required students to design a lesson plan but had to abandon that assignment because lesson plans were so readily available online, which tempted her students to "repurpose" them for her class (also known as plagiarizing). Instead, she asked students to use the Internet to find three lesson plans and write a critique of them. The professor found that student learning improved because of this critical use of Internet materials.

The special nature of the thesis prep course, its student enrollment, and the generalist instructor who typically teaches it also make it amenable to online instruction and discussions in which student viewpoints and personal experiences take center stage. Unlike a lower-division history course where students are expected to learn new material and demonstrate their knowledge on graded examinations and papers, the students in a thesis preparation course are upper-division students, advanced learners who already understand the basics of research, writing, and their major field.

Their experiences, both before and concurrent with the thesis prep course, make their contributions to the class as important as those of the instructor.

In properly designed online courses, students can find themselves seriously engaged, interacting more with other students than they would in a normal classroom situation, and even writing more. Rather than just reading the thesis proposals and completed theses from other students, students can distribute their critiques of these materials online to everyone in the course, perhaps commenting on the strengths and weaknesses they saw, and even incorporating thesis material from other institutions. These critiques can, in turn, be the subject of commentary from other students in the course, just as online articles are followed by readers' comments. And in effect, this semi-public presentation of their work online promotes high-quality work by students as much as any system of grading could.

In addition, in an online discussion forum, students can be prompted to share their personal experiences and viewpoints. They can explain their writing strategies and detail their work plans for the thesis. Just as importantly, they can discuss the problems in research they encounter and the solutions they have discovered. They can be asked to share their experiences finding the right thesis advisor or receiving special assistance for their project from a research librarian. When other students add their comments, their personal experiences, and their strategies, everyone feels that they are engaged in a common endeavor: despite the differences in the topics and plans for thesis projects, they share similar challenges and pressures. This feeling of honors community can also provide a supportive environment that can benefit students' later work on their thesis after completion of the thesis preparation course.

This discussion of online education should not be construed as an argument for abandoning face-to-face classroom instruction and interaction among students and faculty, nor is it intended to argue that the thesis preparation course should be taught online. Online instruction has its drawbacks as well as its advantages, but it is an option that honors directors and deans might seriously consider. At some institutions, the most effective format for a thesis preparation course may be a hybrid course that begins in a classroom, promoting a feeling of honors community and support, then launching thesis students from the classroom into productive relationships with their thesis advisor, and finally using online presentations and discussion to bring together the views and experiences of the thesis students.

The primary objective of any thesis preparation course is not to introduce new subject matter or to test student learning, but to get students started on their thesis work and to have them apply and refine their existing skills and understanding in individualized assignments, presentations to the class, and wide-ranging discussions. Much of their work will be of a preliminary nature, narrowing their ideas for a thesis project, preparing a first draft of a thesis proposal, finding an appropriate faculty advisor, and assembling a preliminary bibliography. Such activities resist traditional grading practices. Hence, grading for this course typically gives great weight to class contributions, participation, and satisfactory completion of assignments. Specifics aside, we strongly believe that some sort of thesis preparation course can be beneficial to students embarking on an honors thesis and that honors programs and colleges should seriously consider offering such support.

CHAPTER 5

Dealing with Common Problems

Certainly honors administrators and faculty do their utmost to support students, and students generally have the best intentions. Nevertheless, things can and do go wrong, regardless of the preparation and support structures in place. Honors directors and deans who take a pragmatic attitude to their thesis programs and are prepared to deal with common problems will have a significant impact on the success of students in the program and the quality of the thesis they complete.

THESIS COMMITMENT PROBLEMS

Most honors program students come more-or-less willingly to thesis work, especially if they have taken a good thesis preparation course. They understand the expectations and the level of commitment a thesis requires, and while they may be somewhat apprehensive about what they see as the magnitude of the work that lies ahead of them, they are nonetheless willing to undertake the challenge. Many students also look forward to working closely with their faculty advisor and doing the independent work that their thesis requires.

Some students, however, are not strongly committed to thesis work. These are not the students who struggle to settle on a thesis topic or narrow it down, nor are they the dropouts who disappear without notice and cut off all contact with the honors program or college. These particular students have met all or most of their other honors program requirements but are now wavering in their commitment to a thesis. Some may just have "senioritis" and want to party or chill out in the time they have left in college before graduation. Others may have serious reservations about undertaking a thesis project rather than foreign study or an internship, or they may not be especially interested in doing in-depth work of any sort. But the majority are just not sure they want to do a thesis and are delaying their commitment until they arrive at some mythical point in the future when everything will become certain, when they discover the right direction to take with their lives, and when they have banished all doubts. Of course, that point may not come until well after graduation.

Honors administrators should recognize that this indecision is frequently a minor version of the larger decision facing a student nearing graduation: "What should I do with my LIFE?" As much as they may have disliked some aspects of college life, it has a comforting predictability to it. An honors thesis requires them, perhaps for the first time, to take a chance, to invest more than one semester in an uncertain product. These perplexities are not signs of intellectual weakness nor a failure of character. The decision about thesis work really is connected to difficult choices that will not have easy or obvious resolutions. Honors program or honors college support for these undecided students is appropriate if not essential. Honors directors, deans, and staff can move them towards discussions that can break the paralysis of indecision and perhaps clarify both the short- and long-term choices they are considering.

A variety of approaches may be necessary here, depending on students' individual circumstances. Many honors deans and directors have found that one of the most useful strategies for dealing with students who have trouble committing to an honors thesis is to help them understand that, in fact, this decision is in most ways similar to other, easier decisions. When students consider going to a new movie, they talk to other students who have seen it. If they were thinking about starting private piano lessons, they would do well to talk with their school music teacher and perhaps experiment by taking a few lessons. Honors programs and colleges should encourage wavering thesis students to take similar small steps forward, although doing so may never banish all their doubts. Scheduling a casual face-to-face discussion about a possible thesis project with a potential thesis advisor can be surprisingly effective. Students often emerge from such meetings with a strong topic, excited about the project, realizing that they are further along in their thinking about a project than they realized, in many ways already engaged in the initial stages of thesis work.

Other students, especially those in majors that require a capstone project or senior research seminar, may also hesitate about undertaking an honors thesis. They frequently believe that thesis-like work in their major should take precedence over an honors thesis. Or they ask, "Why should I do a separate honors thesis when I already have to do a senior project in my major?" Honors directors and deans can help these students see that this situation does not have to be a choice of one or the other. Students do need to complete all the requirements in their majors, but they can frequently combine that work with the honors thesis or use it to form the basis of the thesis. Such arrangements are clearly in accord with the objectives of honors thesis work: encouraging student performance at the highest level. In some honors programs and colleges, a superior thesis written for a departmental senior seminar may be accepted without change as an honors thesis if it satisfies all honors requirements. Other departmental theses or required research projects can easily be rewritten, expanded, or otherwise adapted to meet honors requirements in a 1–2-credit honors thesis course, perhaps with the seminar professor acting as thesis advisor. This supplementary thesis course gives students credit for the extra work they will need to do and records on the students' transcripts the fact that they did an honors thesis.

THE "IRRELEVANT" HONORS THESIS

Some students view the honors thesis not for its value in itself, but as a stepping-stone to their future. This same perspective prompts some high school seniors to slack off after they have been accepted into a college or university. Similarly, an honors thesis may seem unnecessary or irrelevant once students have been accepted into graduate and professional schools or have a good job offer in hand. Students in this situation should be congratulated, then reminded that work on an honors thesis is actually relevant to their plans for study or work after graduation. Students who complete an honors thesis usually find that they are better prepared for graduate school, for professional school, and for work in their chosen careers than are their equally bright classmates who have not experienced the challenge of independent thesis work.

Some students believe that an honors thesis is just another academic exercise with little payoff and little value for the real-world activities they envision in their future. Students in some career paths, such as business, criminal justice, and other practical or pre-professional areas, have particular trouble seeing the relevance of thesis work. Honors administrators need to point out that a thesis will demonstrate to employers that the student is willing and able to do more than meet minimal requirements. A successfully completed thesis underscores that the student is not afraid of challenges and rises to meet them. Finishing a thesis exemplifies a student's capacity for independent work and a commitment to carrying sizable projects to completion. Just as importantly, a thesis demonstrates that the student has the research, writing, and presentation skills others may lack, as well as effective organizational and time-management skills. Moreover, while a high GPA indicates potential for the future, honors thesis work is clearly a more practical demonstration of the intellectual abilities and work skills that the students will bring to their jobs and develop in their careers. An honors thesis demonstrates not just what the students can do but what they actually have done.

TROUBLE FINDING A THESIS ADVISOR

Selecting a thesis advisor may be the most important decision students make about their thesis work, perhaps even more important than the thesis topic. A well-chosen thesis advisor can help students settle on a thesis topic, refine it, and complete a quality thesis in a timely fashion. And a well-chosen thesis advisor can help to ensure that thesis work leads not just to a completed thesis project, but also to a valuable undergraduate experience.

Most students avoid major problems in finding the right advisor by selecting a faculty member from whom they have already taken a class. These faculty have a good idea about the student's abilities, intellectual promise, and work ethic, so they are usually willing to take on a thesis student they know well. The student will have a good idea of this faculty member's perspectives, research interests, and performance expectations. This familiarity is a good basis for an effective mentoring relationship and productive thesis work. On the other hand, a student will sometimes want to work with a particular faculty member just "because he's a good guy," even though the faculty member has no expertise in the area of the student's thesis project. At this point, an honors director or dean may want to direct the student to another, more appropriate, potential advisor rather than face the possibility of inadequate faculty guidance and poor thesis work. (This problem is an example of the kind of issues that a thesis prep course can address.)

At times, a potential thesis advisor will turn a student down, or a student will be unable to find a faculty member in a relevant area. If the student has no backup plan, this experience can be devastating. Honors administrators and staff need to be there for the student to discuss alternative thesis topics or other possible advisors. Having an honors dean or director with good contacts on campus and a strong knowledge of faculty interests and campus resources will help. Having this knowledge and these connections provides a strong reason for selecting honors deans and directors from the seasoned faculty at an institution. In these cases, the honors dean or director may want to contact a faculty member or the department chair in advance to let him or her know that an honors thesis student is coming to talk about selecting a thesis advisor. Not only can these meetings elicit other suggestions for possible thesis topics and advisors, but they can also make more faculty aware of the honors thesis program.

Whether the potential thesis advisor is someone the student knows well or not at all, the student should be told to set up a face-to-face discussion of his or her ideas for a thesis. Notes in faculty mailboxes, thesis proposals slipped under office doors, vague voice-mail messages, and emails are ineffective. Faculty may overlook or forget to respond to students' email or voicemail. Moreover, faculty who do not wish to take on the responsibility of thesis advisement are tempted to ignore impersonal requests. Even willing and interested faculty members usually need to know more about a student's ideas for a thesis. Therefore, most potential thesis advisors want to have a face-to-face discussion with the student about the proposed project before they will agree to direct the student's thesis.

The honors dean or director should encourage students to set up formal appointments with faculty for the discussion of a thesis project, not just to run up to them between classes or unexpectedly drop in on them during office hours. Students should be encouraged to look respectable, not necessarily ready for the business world, but in a way that communicates maturity and seriousness. They should come prepared at least with a general idea for their thesis, a direction, or a topic. "Something about the Reformation, maybe on Martin Luther's political views" is a good starting point. "I have no idea, but I was hoping you'd tell me" sounds unthoughtful and leads nowhere. Students should understand that the faculty member can help them focus on a topic or area and refine their ideas but is usually reluctant to make the decisions for them. Potential thesis advisors may also have questions for them, such as how they became interested in an area or topic, what preparation they have, and what approaches most interest them. In short, students should be made fully aware that the thesis and their work with a thesis advisor require a professional approach and discussion.

THE NONTRADITIONAL THESIS

Most honors students will choose to undertake a thesis in their major discipline. This decision is not surprising: the thesis is intended to be the culminating experience for students who have spent several years progressing from general education courses to specializing in a major. Honors deans, directors, and faculty advisors are very familiar with this type of thesis. A strong case exists, however, for allowing, even encouraging, honors thesis students to move outside the comfort zone of their major. Certainly students should not tackle projects for which they are completely unprepared. For instance, a student who has taken no creative writing courses should not be encouraged to write a novel as a thesis project, and that student will likely have serious difficulty finding a faculty advisor. Some students do have both the interest and the skills that would enable them to use their theses to explore an area outside their major and be successful.

Some honors programs and colleges have a strong interdisciplinary emphasis that they want their students to adopt in their thesis work. But even without such a programmatic interdisciplinary emphasis, many honors students have a broad range of interests, are double majors, or have one or more minors or certifications they hope to complete in addition to their major. Some may also plan to enter graduate school or professional fields in an area different from their majors. A knowledgeable honors director or dean can steer students who wish to pursue an interdisciplinary or multidisciplinary thesis project to faculty who not only have the skills and background needed, but who also are familiar with interdisciplinary work, are used to working with other faculty on an honors thesis, or are open to explorations off the beaten path.

By way of example, one honors director met with a student who was completely confused about where her thesis should reside. She was a double major in English and Secondary Education, with a Theatre minor. All perfectly logical if she planned to teach high school English. The student mentioned that she had become more and more interested in theatre tech, but did not know if it would be possible for an English major to do a thesis in this area. After a lengthy discussion with the honors director, the student felt comfortable focusing on the technical aspects of producing Shakespeare's plays, and the director was able to guide her to several possible thesis advisors in the English and Theatre departments, two of whom readily agreed to work with her. Ultimately, it did not matter which department the advisors were from; their interest in and commitment to the thesis was the most important thing. Without the input of the honors administrator, the student would have been too intimidated and frustrated to pursue a thesis.

If the honors thesis requires only one advisor, that advisor should be a faculty member in the thesis project's dominant discipline or a faculty member open to interdisciplinary projects. When a student has more than one thesis advisor, the director or dean can help students select advisors representing different perspectives and help set up productive working relationships. The student and the participating faculty must know which faculty advisor is primary, how the student will keep the advisors up to date on thesis progress, how the faculty will provide input concerning the student's work, what the possibilities are for joint meetings, when various parts of the thesis will be turned in to the different advisors, and who will be responsible for thesis grading and approval.

Sometimes, a student will want to write a thesis on an unusual topic, one that does not fit neatly into any major. For example, several years ago one of the authors had a student whose major was zoology but who wanted to write his honors thesis on the history of the yo-yo. He had been a lifelong yo-yo enthusiast and wanted to learn more about it. But why not write his thesis in zoology? Quite simply, because he wanted to take a break from his highly focused curriculum to explore another interest. The advice given to the student: if he could find a faculty member willing to work with him, the honors program would also support his thesis. The outcome was a marvelous thesis. He brought the knowledge, insights, and research skills he had developed in his zoology major, as well as his other coursework, to his yo-yo study. (Did you know that yo-yoers refer to those of us who are not yo-yo aficionados as "Yuggles"?)

The moral of this story has wide application for honors directors and deans involved in guiding their students into good thesis work: trust the honors education that students have experienced, be open and imaginative, and support their new paths and desires as much as possible. For some students, the honors thesis is a great opportunity to dig deep into a specific area of their major. For others, the honors thesis may be a great opportunity for an intellectual adventure, risky though that may seem to some faculty. If not now, then when? Ultimately, deciding on what might be an appropriate thesis project comes down to the kind of honors experience that honors deans and directors value and what they are willing to permit or promote in their thesis programs.

INCORPORATING INTERNSHIPS AND PRE-PROFESSIONAL EXPERIENCES

Honors directors and deans also need to pay special attention to students in professional majors, such as business, education, the sciences, and engineering, as well as those students in other majors that require or encourage internships. Students in these areas who want to produce a thesis may find doing so difficult because of the extensive requirements and tight structure of their majors. Often, an honors director or dean can help these students and their faculty understand how major requirements and activities can become a sound basis for an honors thesis. For instance, students in education could conduct what education professors call "action research" in their student-teaching classroom and then include this experience and data in their thesis. Students in engineering and the sciences often have a required capstone project or are working in research teams on projects that could be the basis for an honors thesis. Students in business often have internships or off-campus work experiences that could be the nuclei of an honors thesis project or could function in other ways in an honors thesis.

It must be admitted that for many faculty, the preparation and research practices associated with the traditional thesis in the liberal arts would seem to rule out these practical or real-world experiences. If an honors program or college hopes to encourage more theses in professional areas, the honors director or dean will frequently need to make it clear to both students and faculty that an honors thesis that incorporates these activities is both possible and desirable. For example, internships sometimes require extensive written, analytical reports that could serve as the basis for an honors thesis. At other times, the internship experience has been so significant that the students are eager to use and expand on it in their thesis. A more difficult task may be finding a sympathetic advisor who can guide them in such hybrid thesis work.

The honors administrator, in consultation with the faculty advisor, must take care to ensure that students receive the appropriate credit when they combine an internship with thesis work. Perhaps the student could bring the internship report up to honors thesis level by some additional library research, a tighter experimental focus, more extensive data analysis, or the addition of self-reflective comments that would not require the normal 3–4-credit thesis course, but only a 1–2-credit thesis course.

Any plan to increase honors thesis production in such areas must involve the cooperation and assistance of the faculty in relevant professional areas. The task is not always easy: faculty members may have limited experience with honors thesis work in their disciplines or inflexible views about what thesis work can and should be. They may believe that their students lack the time for a thesis, that their curriculum is not amenable to a thesis, or even that thesis work would add little of value to an undergraduate's career in their discipline. Furthermore, many faculty in liberal arts disciplines have great difficulty imagining how a student could incorporate internships and other off-campus experiences into a solid honors thesis.

We know of no perfect argument that will convince skeptical faculty that such theses are both appropriate and valuable. But such thesis work does exemplify a central and compelling insight about the value of education: both the realm of thought and the realm of experience are necessary for understanding the world fully. Study, research, and thoughtful analysis often arise from the close observation of real-world events and behaviors, and basic research frequently leads to practical applications. If an honors thesis can accommodate the intertwined and interdependent realms of both thought and action, so much the better.

LATE ARRIVALS TO A MAJOR

Recent transfer students, students who settle on a major late in their college careers, and students who have recently changed majors often face special problems in selecting a thesis topic or advisor. They may not know many faculty in their new department, and they may not yet have had the advanced coursework in the major that is necessary to create a sound thesis proposal. The faculty in their department may also be reluctant to take on a student they have never taught, whose previous work in the discipline might have been done at another institution, or whose ideas about a thesis project seem unfocused and uninformed. The setbacks and frustrations these students encounter as they attempt to begin their thesis work may prompt many of them to give up on the honors thesis before they even find an advisor.

If honors directors or deans wish to help these late arrivals succeed, they must address such problems directly. Students in these situations need to know that they may have to approach several faculty members to discuss various thesis options, including topics that may differ markedly from the students' initial ideas. These students need to be especially open and flexible when considering a thesis topic, possibly even becoming involved in a faculty member's own research. Like late arrivals to the cafeteria, they need to select from what is available.

Students also need to know that if their initial efforts are unsuccessful, the honors director and staff are there to assist them. Honors directors and deans can identify sympathetic and helpful faculty in the student's major or point the student to faculty who in the past have demonstrated their willingness and ability to work with new majors to refine their ideas for a thesis. Honors directors and deans can do much to help students through these difficult experiences by pointing out that secondary choices for both advisors and thesis topics can still lead to rewarding thesis experiences. The value of the honors thesis will come primarily from the thesis process, from successful thesis work, not from a specific project.

FACULTY INPUT ON THESIS PROPOSALS AND WORK PLANS

An honors director or dean should help all thesis students understand that a good thesis advisor is reluctant to simply rubber stamp the student's proposal. Faculty advisors are more likely than not to ask students to rework and refine their initial proposal for the project. This request can come as quite a shock to students who are not prepared for additional work and a high level of faculty involvement in the production of a final document. Yet it can also be a valuable reality check: thesis work is an evolving process, very different from submitting completed course assignments for faculty grading or approval, with nothing further expected from the student. In thesis work a continual give-and-take between faculty advisors and thesis students will enable students to perform at their highest level.

This exchange is the essence of the mentoring relationship and an indispensable aspect of honors thesis work. First and foremost, it can help students avoid potential obstacles and direct their efforts to thesis work that is more likely to be successful. Because of their own research experiences, faculty members understand the need for a work plan that is correctly focused, carefully organized, and realistic in its scope. They also want to ensure that the thesis is appropriate for the resources available to the student and can be completed within the time constraints. Obviously, students producing a thesis must take the first few steps on their own, formulating their initial ideas and securing an advisor. But as soon as thesis students appear in their offices, good faculty advisors will work closely with them at each step of the thesis process, from proposal and work plan through to the final product.

Students and their thesis advisors must have a clear understanding of the thesis requirements and the step-by-step process that they need to follow for successful completion of the thesis. Honors administrators should encourage faculty advisors to review thesis requirements and supplementary material with their thesis students: sharing an understanding of the tasks ahead is a prerequisite for a strong working relationship between advisor and student.

Regular meetings are also a necessity, perhaps every other week, with the advisor and the student suggesting specific tasks and expectations for these meetings. Without this scheduling, meetings between advisors and students may be unfocused and unproductive, thesis work may get bogged down, faculty and students may find it difficult to work last-minute meetings into their busy schedules, and guilty students may avoid contact with their advisor because they have completed little work. A few honors programs ask students to submit their work plans to the honors program or college, but most rely on faculty advisors to establish good schedules and performance deadlines with their students. Some honors programs, however, require students whose thesis projects stretch over two semesters or more to submit progress reports of some sort to the honors program, indicating that their thesis work is proceeding well and meeting with the faculty advisor's approval.

Honors directors and deans should help students recognize that even with this faculty input, the students themselves bear the major responsibility for completing the thesis. Students should also understand that they bear some responsibility for making the mentoring relationship as successful as possible. Sometimes students will need to steer discussions with their advisors to focus more specifically on the problems they have encountered or the questions they have about future work. They should not be afraid to ask follow-up questions to clarify their advisor's suggestions; they may even have to suggest extra meetings with their advisor to address significant issues in their thesis work. Honors directors and deans should encourage students to speak up for themselves with their advisor and to be candid about their concerns.

Students should expect their advisor to both encourage and cajole them as they work through their thesis project, but students should not expect an advisor to do their thesis work for them. If students fall behind in their work, miss meetings with their thesis advisor, fail to follow directions suggested by their advisor, and miss important deadlines, it is the students who are responsible for lack of success with their thesis. In such cases of inadequate student performance, when well-intentioned thesis advisors may throw up their hands in frustration, honors administrators must let the faculty know that the honors program or college supports their judgment and will back their efforts to deal with the situation.

MIDTERM STUDENT SLUMPS

Some students begin the honors thesis with the best intentions, work diligently at it for a while, and then come to a halt, perhaps believing that they will be able to pull it out with extra effort in the last few weeks of school. Sometimes students feel overwhelmed by the extracurricular demands of senior year, especially the tasks related to applying to graduate school or finding a job. Sometimes their interest in their thesis topic wanes, or they are just tired of all the work. Whatever the reason for this crisis point, the student must recognize that a great deal is at stake. Unless the student can recover from the slump, the thesis may remain uncompleted, putting the student's graduation at risk.

If an honors program or college is serious about providing personalized education that supports student performance at the highest levels, active intervention is warranted at this point. Some students need a prod from the honors director or dean as well as from their thesis advisor, especially if they have lost confidence in their abilities and need support and encouragement. Other students may need some time off. The task of the honors dean or director is sometimes just to calm and reassure the student, perhaps suggesting that he or she spend a bit of time away from the pressure of the thesis and then re-engage in thesis work with revived commitment. None of these strategies will guarantee success, but sometimes just knowing that people are trying to help enables a floundering and exhausted student to pull his or her act together and progress to a successful finish.

THE HONORS PROGRAM'S RESPONSIBILITIES FOR THESIS ADVISEMENT

Honors directors, deans, and staff should consider themselves as backup advisors for all thesis students whenever faculty or students need them. Many programs and colleges maintain regular contact with thesis students and their advisors as a part of the oversight procedures for their thesis programs. Both students and faculty usually appreciate the interest the honors program or college takes in the progress of their thesis work. Experienced honors directors and deans also know that they need to be alert to early warnings of potential problems rather than letting problems or inadequacies suddenly emerge at the end of a semester when little can be done.

Calling individual students in for discussions of their thesis work; bringing thesis students together in small groups to talk about their thesis experiences; requiring regular progress reports; or using email, course management software, or social media to allow students to share their thesis experiences, and especially their problems, are effective oversight procedures used in many programs. Thesis students may be too embarrassed to mention their own problems, but they may open up in response to the problems other students are having in their thesis work, their personal lives, or their relationships with their advisor.

Often, the honors dean or director can reinforce the faculty advisor's suggestions, pose effective alternatives, or simply buck up the self-confidence of students so they can work their way over or around obstacles. Honors deans and directors understand both the difficulties of thesis research and the difficulties that can arise in working with faculty. Sometimes their perspective provides a clear path forward for students. At other times, the honors director or dean may need to talk with the thesis advisor directly about problems that come up, even if they are not directly connected to the advisor. When such discussions with an advisor are not productive, the honors director may need to call on a department chair for assistance, advice, or suggestions about other options that may be available. These scenarios may not result in a superior thesis, but they can result in a credible and completed thesis.

Occasionally, the mentoring relationship breaks down. Thesis advisors sometimes fail to meet their commitments to the student and the thesis work. Faculty may be overextended; they may routinely forget meetings; they may experience a family crisis or illness. But whatever the reason, if faculty advisors are unable to provide adequate guidance and support, they may leave students hanging in the midst of their thesis work, or in limbo at the end of a thesis draft, with little idea of what, if anything, they should do.

At other times, serious conflicts can develop between advisors and their thesis student, often because of poor communication. The student may feel that the faculty member has not provided clear guidance or has changed his or her expectations. Perhaps the faculty member feels that he or she has been forthcoming, but that the student has disregarded the advice, failed to do the hard work necessary, or simply produced inferior work. In some cases, the advisor may have graduate-level expectations that are inappropriate for an undergraduate thesis. Any number of scenarios present themselves, and the honors administrator may face challenges in sorting through the problems, let alone in solving them.

In such situations, the honors deans or directors can try to mediate between student and advisor to resolve the major issues. Honors directors and deans should feel comfortable consulting department chairs and enlisting their assistance. Department chairs have a vested interest in making the thesis process work well because both the student and advisor are usually in the same department. Sometimes replacing the advisor may be possible, and that change will enable the student to bring the thesis work to a successful conclusion. At other times, especially when the student's work is inadequate, a successful honors thesis may have become an impossibility.

Honors deans and directors can easily get caught between a rock and a hard place, but the principles that need to be followed are quite simple. When students mess up, they must deal with the consequences; when the institution or its designated faculty advisors are partially at fault, the institution and its representatives must deal with the consequences. Department chairs and especially honors directors and deans are clearly the institution's representatives when it comes to honors theses. Ultimately, the buck stops with the honors director.

THESIS QUALITY

All honors administrators and thesis advisors expect, or at least hope for, theses of the highest quality. They want to encourage the student to produce a superior thesis that reflects well on the student, on the advisor, on the honors program, and on the institution. But what constitutes "highest quality" or "superior work"? Honors theses do vary in quality, and there are huge differences in the theses produced in different disciplines, including methodology, sources, extent of originality, and even thesis length. For many honors directors, striving for theses of the "highest quality" or "honors quality" may be another case of "I can't define it, but I know it when I see it."

But what about the thesis that does not live up to this indefinable standard? What about the student who works diligently, who meets regularly with his or her advisor, who does all the right things, yet still produces an "average" undergraduate thesis, a thesis that would perhaps deserve a C+? Should the honors directors accept this work as an honors thesis?

The answer seems to depend on the philosophy of the honors college or program. If the belief is that only the best and the brightest should survive, then an "average" thesis by an honors program student will not qualify as an honors thesis at some institutions. Other honors programs and colleges, however, have adopted a different philosophy, the Chinese philosophy famously adopted by Steve Jobs: the journey is the reward. If the student has worked hard and grown intellectually through thesis work, and if the thesis meets format, bibliographical, and other honors program requirements, perhaps it should be accepted for what it is: not a superior piece of work but an adequate one. We are not suggesting that honors programs should accept whatever gets thrown at them; a thesis with incomplete work, inadequate research, sloppy writing, or simpleminded analysis is unacceptable and should be given back to the student and advisor for repair or even rejection. We are suggesting, however, that honors deans and directors should consider a range in quality for the honors thesis, which may extend from Acceptable to Very Good to Excellent.

An honors administrator can respond to issues of quality in a variety of ways while still maintaining the integrity of the honors thesis program. As a first step, the honors director or dean must be realistic about the variations in honors thesis quality and the grades that students deserve for their work. Just like students in lower-division honors courses, some thesis students do not do "A" work. While a student may not appreciate receiving a lower grade on the thesis, it is sometimes warranted, perhaps even a grade lower than a "B." As a second step, the honors director or dean should determine the context and the reasons for the student's poor work; because the thesis comes at the conclusion of a student's undergraduate career, conventional responses to unsatisfactory performance may not be sufficient.

THESIS GRADING AND THESIS APPROVAL

The thesis grading and approval process is likely to proceed without a hitch for students who do clearly superior thesis work. They receive an "A" for their thesis, thesis advisors brag to their colleagues about the work of their students, and the finished theses are submitted to the honors program or college as obviously exceptional pieces of work that satisfy all the honors requirements.

But more often than deans and directors would like to admit, something goes wrong in the mentoring/evaluation/approval process. The result is not only an inferior honors thesis but one that the faculty advisor seems to have approved and graded without much scrutiny. Advisors have heavy workloads at the end of each term, and some are tempted to provide only a cursory reading of the final thesis. Their previous work with the student can lead them to assume that this final work will be good enough. Sometimes thesis advisors give students a social pass, not wanting to impede the graduation of otherwise worthy students who have submitted a thesis that is substandard or defective in one way or another. Such problems are messy, and they are problems that can literally land on the honors director's desk without warning in the last hours of a semester.

Some honors directors and deans believe that they can and should do nothing at this point. The responsibility for the grading and approval of thesis work is vested in the thesis advisors. Honors directors, deans, and their staff should not act like arrogant polymaths, thrusting their way into normal faculty evaluation procedures, insisting that their judgment is better than that of faculty experts. Moreover, it is now too late for an honors dean or director to do anything constructive.

Other deans and directors believe that honors approval should be more than passive silence and acquiescence. They and their staff read or skim all honors theses. They believe that they can and should insist on acceptable thesis work because an honors thesis is not just a matter of faculty grading: this evaluation reflects institutional and honors program standards. One need not be a rocket scientist to notice that a student thesis on rocket science is poorly written, has some pages out of order or missing, or is lacking both the required bibliography and a section of reflective commentary. These honors directors and deans believe that they cannot in good conscience act for the institution in certifying such a thesis until it meets honors standards for approval.

Even though students may have left the campus and faculty may be engaged in other projects or activities, sometimes the student can improve the thesis, especially if the tasks to do so are reasonable, such as a more thorough proofreading, the compilation or reworking of a bibliography, or the preparation of a section of student reflections. Sometimes an honors director or dean can contact the student directly to have these tasks completed before honors program approval and imprimatur can be granted. But in a few cases where the student needs to make major improvements, the honors administrator should also involve the faculty advisor. Sometimes the advisor alone will be effective in having the thesis bought up to acceptable standards.

When problems with the quality of a thesis arise—whether rooted in poor proofreading or in more serious problems such as sloppy writing, inadequate research, unprofessional documentation—an honors director or dean is wise to invoke the public nature of thesis work as the rationale for required thesis revisions. No one wants to be associated with a shoddy thesis, and faculty advisors are understandably concerned about their professional reputations. Because an honors thesis becomes a public document when digitally archived or placed in an institutional library, other students and departmental faculty are likely to see it. Rather than directly criticizing or challenging the faculty advisor's evaluation of the thesis, experienced honors deans and directors often position themselves as allies of the faculty member by suggesting changes in the thesis that would better reflect the true quality of the thesis advisor's efforts.

Finally, the honors director or dean should not forget the obligation of the honors program or college to help students through difficulties whenever possible. Sometimes illness or injuries handicap student performance, sometimes fires destroy laboratories and research notes, and a wide variety of other factors can impede a student's thesis work. In these rare cases, exploring compromise options is sometimes advisable. Would it not be appropriate in some cases to give a student who suffered a serious accident in the middle of the semester partial credit for the thesis work completed or to reconfigure a thesis course into an independent study that does not require rigorous review and approval by the honors program or college? Just as good students can sometimes write a bad thesis, so bad things can happen to good students. As a general rule, honors deans, directors, and their programs should be supportive of both students and faculty while still promoting the highest levels of student work.

Some Final Words

Most of the time an honors thesis program operates smoothly: honors thesis work encourages both faculty and students to work at their highest level, and impressive theses appear with regularity. At other times, however, an honors thesis program seems to be like a Pandora's box: new problems, conflicts, and strains emerge as often as the weather changes. It does not take long for an honors administrator to experience both the highs and lows of running an honors program, and especially an honors thesis program. We have based this handbook on the strong conviction that honors theses have great value, not only for the students who complete them but also for the honors programs, the colleges, and the universities that sponsor them. The focus on best practices and options in this handbook is intended to help honors directors and deans improve their individual thesis programs.

The honors thesis has had a growing impact on undergraduate education in general. It has offered a clear model for the expansion of undergraduate research opportunities and for the introduction of departmental or institution-wide thesis projects for non-honors students. The honors thesis has demonstrated the capacity of undergraduates to undertake and complete independent work successfully, and today the academic world has expanded the number of opportunities for such work to students and disciplines that traditional theses had not previously reached. Barriers between programs of study and barriers to undergraduate research have begun to break down. Thesis preparation courses are being added in many departments, as are courses that engage students in ongoing faculty research (not to be confused with research methods courses or independent study courses). Finally, the value of such work in an undergraduate's career has led more and more institutions to require a thesis or similar project from a growing number of students.

Similarly, the faculty-student mentoring model inherent in the honors thesis process has had an impact on undergraduate education as a whole. Faculty mentoring of honors theses, as well as the seminar setting for many honors courses, has both demonstrated and promoted the value of personalized student-faculty interactions in undergraduate education. Institutions have identified a broader range of faculty, not just senior tenure-track faculty engaged in research or creative projects, as having the potential to be excellent mentors for undergraduate thesis students. In addition, institutions clearly encourage and support their faculty in mentoring independent research and creative activities at every level of undergraduate study. Faculty mentors encourage their students to make presentations at the special programs and undergraduate research days held on many campuses. They also lead their students beyond the local campus into active participation in NCHC, NCUR, and regional honors conferences, or at the conferences in many academic disciplines, which now provide undergraduates with other opportunities to present and publish their work.

The institutional value of an honors thesis program and the important role played by the honors dean or director became increasingly apparent as our examination progressed. In the operation of a thesis program, the honors dean or director maintains contacts across the campus with a wide variety of disciplines and with an expanding number of thesis advisors and department chairs. These connections can lead to new honors classes and can attract new faculty to enhance honors offerings. A typical pattern in honors is that a faculty member who has been at the institution for a few years gets an opportunity to work as a thesis advisor with an honors student. The rewarding nature of this experience often prompts the professor to volunteer to teach an honors course and to pursue opportunities to offer research and mentoring experiences to other majors in the department. This situation is win-win for everyone involved.

As colleges and universities seek to demonstrate the high quality of their educational programs through the assessment of student learning, the honors thesis can become a model for evaluating undergraduate education as a whole. Because the honors thesis is a capstone project that brings together a student's general education coursework and advanced studies in the major, the thesis becomes an excellent reflection of an undergraduate's entire academic career. Consequently, the honors thesis is increasingly used as a central document in assessing undergraduate learning by honors programs as well as by individual departments and the institution as a whole. With the pressures for assessment and certification so prevalent in the current academic world, capstone projects such as the honors thesis are likely to become more widespread.

We have found that just as honors programs and colleges are not cookie-cutter, one-size-fits-all creatures, neither are honors theses or the honors thesis programs that support them. Like the honors program itself, thesis requirements and programs must mesh with the institution's overall mission, vision, goals, and resources. Some honors programs and colleges are committed to offering a thesis preparation course; some cannot and do not; and at some institutions the thesis preparation may fall within the purview of departments. Some programs will require students to have several thesis advisors; some will be comfortable with one, while others will require the thesis to be vetted by a faculty committee.

Honors thesis programs also differ in the role the honors program or college plays in thesis work. Some honors programs and their institutions require a particular thesis format, length, and approach; other institutions leave that decision to the thesis advisor, the student's department, or the student's college. Some honors programs and departments provide funding for thesis research while others cannot. And in some institutions, such as two-year colleges, a thesis simply may not be feasible. What works extremely well at one institution may be problematic at another. Tailoring the thesis to the program and institution, not to a particular paradigm, is the key to a thriving and successful thesis program. Likewise, significant institutional variations exist in the role the honors director or dean plays or is able to play in the thesis process. Even if honors directors or deans are reluctant to act as the ultimate arbiters of quality work, they must be willing and able to deal with the vast differences in honors theses.

Honors directors and deans also need to be realistic. Not everything will work out as well as it was intended. Conflicts between advisor and student will arise. An advisor may, at the last moment, receive a grant and go on leave, forcing the student to find a new advisor. A student's thesis funding may fall through; the mentoring relationship with the faculty advisor may be subverted by the student's failures, absences, and lame excuses; or the student may simply produce a weak thesis. The honors director or dean must be prepared to deal with situations such as these in a timely fashion.

It is clear that some students will fail to complete a thesis despite all the pointers for sound thesis work on honors websites, all the advice in honors handbooks, the numerous handouts distributed to students and faculty, the sound design of a thesis prep course, and the dedication of thesis advisors and honors staff. This unfortunate situation is simply a fact of life and is often largely out of the honors director's control. Hence, the goals of the honors director should be pragmatic: to increase thesis completion rates, to improve honors program and college retention, and to demonstrate to students that they can be successful at advanced, independent work.

We hope that this handbook will offer some guidance when the inevitable problems arise in the thesis process. We hope as well that honors directors and deans will see that most of the problems they encounter are not unique to their institution, that others in their position have often found effective solutions to these difficulties, and that their peers at other institutions can be excellent sources of advice. Other honors directors and deans are usually extremely generous with their time and are happy to share their experiences. In addition, many honors program and honors college websites offer thesis handbooks or web pages with detailed advice about the thesis. Certainly looking at other institutions that are comparable in size and structure is likely to be helpful, but exploring the honors thesis programs at a variety of institutions can be equally beneficial.

As we have said repeatedly, the honors thesis represents the institution's highest level of undergraduate achievement. Honors deans and directors facilitate this superior work by helping students mold vague ideas into a viable thesis, by helping both students and faculty make the thesis experience rewarding, and by providing the institution with a model and a method to maximize excellence. Encouraging undergraduate work at the highest level is the ultimate justification for honors thesis programs and why we, along with so many others, have chosen to work in honors education.

SELECTED BIBLIOGRAPHY

Albritton, Frank P., Jr. "Humboldt's Unity of Research and Teaching: Influence on the Philosophy and Development of U.S. Higher Education." *Social Science Research Network* 24 Oct. 2006. Web. <http://dx.doi.org/10.2139/ssrn.939811>.

Andrews, Larry. R. *Fundrai$ing for Honor$: A Handbook*. Lincoln: National Collegiate Honors Council, NCHC Monograph Series, 2009. Print.

Aydelotte, Frank. *Breaking the Lock Step: The Development of Honors Work in American Colleges and Universities*. New York: Harper, 1944. Print.

Beard, Jennifer, Ryan D. Shelton, Amanda Stevens, George H. Swindell IV, and Raymond J. Green. "Student-Guided Thesis Support Groups." *HIP* 6 (2010): 69–72. Print.

Breimer, Douwe D., and Bibliotheek der Rijksuniversiteit (Leiden), et. al. *Hora Est !: On Dissertations*. Leiden: Universiteitsbibliotheek, 2005. Print.

Briggs, Kaitlin A. "Thesis as Rhizome: A New Vision for the Honors Thesis in the Twenty-First Century." *JNCHC* 10.2 (2009): 103–114. Print.

Buckner, Ellen B. "Ten Steps to Honors Publication: How Students Can Prepare Their Honors Work for Publication." *HIP* 3 (2007): 149–155. Print.

Camille, Michael. *Image on the Edge: The Margins of Medieval Art*. London: Reaktion Books, 2013. Print.

Campbell, K. Celeste. "The Perceived Value of Honors Work as It Relates to Faculty Promotion and Tenure." *JNCHC* 4.1 (2003): 13–25. Print.

Coey, Aaron T., and Carolyn Haynes. "Honors Pre-Thesis Workshop, 2.0." *HIP* 8 (2012): 109–131. Print.

Cordero, Minerva, Theresa Jorgensen, and Barbara A. Shipman. "Designing Independent Honors Projects in Mathematics." *The Other Culture: Science and Mathematics Education in Honors.* Ed. Ellen B. Buckner and Keith Garbutt. Lincoln: National Collegiate Honors Council, 2012. 185–196. NCHC Monograph Series. Print.

Corley, Christopher R., and John Zubizarreta. "The Power and Utility of Reflective Learning Portfolios in Honors." *JNCHC* 13.1 (2012): 63–76. Print.

Cundall, Michael. "Service Learning and Skunkworks in a Senior Honors Colloquium." *HIP* 6 (2010): 117–123. Print.

Cundall, Michael K., Jr. "How to Develop and Promote an Undergraduate Research Day." *HIP* 2 (2006): 49–57. Print.

Daly, Lowrie J. *The Medieval University, 1200–1400.* New York: Sheed and Ward, 1961. Print.

DiLauro, Alyce, Teron Meyers, and Laura Guertin. "The Value of Extending the Honors Contract Beyond One Semester: A Case Study with Smithsonian Dinosaurs." *HIP* 6 (2010): 109–115. Print.

Doran, Michael. "Honors Senior Theses Are ABET Friendly: Developing a Process to Meet Accreditation Requirements." *The Other Culture: Science and Mathematics Education in Honors.* Ed. Ellen B. Buckner and Keith Garbutt. Lincoln: National Collegiate Honors Council, 2012. 197–206. NCHC Monograph Series. Print.

Dunbar, David, Melissa Terlecki, Nancy Watterson, and Lisa Ratmansky. "An Honors Interdisciplinary Community-Based Research Course." *HIP* 9 (2013): 129–140. Print.

Eble, Kenneth E., ed. *Fostering Academic Excellence Through Honors Programs.* San Francisco: Jossey-Bass, 1986. Print.

Elgren, Tim, and Nancy Hensel. "Undergraduate Research Experiences: Synergies between Scholarship and Teaching." *Peer Review* 8.1 (2006): 4–7. Print.

Estess, Ted L. "Honors Scholarship: Another View." *JNCHC* 5.1 (2004): 25–27. Print.

Fields, Joyce. "Using External Review in the Honors Project Process." *HIP* 4 (2008): 155–161. Print.

Gardner, John N., Gretchen Van Der Veer, and Associates. *The Senior Year Experience: Facilitating Reflection, Integration, Closure and Transition.* San Francisco: Jossey-Bass, 1998. Print.

Gustafson, Kevin, and Zachary Cureton. "Re-Envisioning the Honors Senior Project: Experience as Research." *HIP* 10 (2014): 55–70. Print.

Guzy, Annmarie. *Honors Composition: Historical Perspectives and Contemporary Practices.* Lincoln: National Collegiate Honors Council, NCHC Monograph Series, 2003. Print.

Haggerty, Mark, Theodore Coladarci, Mimi Killinger, and Charlie Slavin. "Honors Thesis Rubrics: A Step toward More Consistent and Valid Assessment in Honors." *JNCHC* 12.2 (2011): 145–166. Print.

Haskins, Charles Homer. *The Rise of Universities.* Ithaca: Cornell UP, 1957. Print.

Henscheid, Jean M. *Professing the Disciplines: An Analysis of Senior Seminars and Capstone Courses.* Columbia, SC: U of South Carolina, National Resource Center for The First-Year Experience and Students in Transition, 2000. Print.

Hilberg, Nathan. "Is Originality an Appropriate Requirement for Undergraduate Publication?" *HIP* 6 (2010): 57–60. Print.

Hilberg, Nathan, and Jaclyn Bankert. "Extra Breadth and Depth in Undergraduate Education: The Institutional Impact of an Interdisciplinary Honors Research Fellowship." *JNCHC* 12.2 (2011): 75–77. Print.

Kimball, Bruce A. "Toward Pragmatic Liberal Education." *The Condition of Liberal Education*. Ed. Robert Orrill. New York: College Board, 1995. Print.

Lacey, Jim. "The Senior Honors Thesis: From Millstone to Capstone." *HIP* 4 (2008): 143–144. Print.

Levinson, Julie, and Richard Mandel. "Teaching Research Methodologies to Professionally Oriented Honors Students." *HIP* 9 (2013): 163–172. Print.

Levy, Foster, Rebecca Pyles, Celia Szarejko, and Linda Wyatt. "Developing an Electronic Repository for Undergraduate Theses." *HIP* 8 (2012): 135–146. Print.

Light, Richard J. *Making the Most of College: Students Speak Their Minds*. Cambridge: Harvard UP, 2004. Print.

Lipson, Charles. *How to Write a BA Thesis*. Chicago: U of Chicago P, 2005. Print.

Markus, Lisa, Jill McKinney, and Anne M. Wilson. "Exploring the Synergies between Undergraduate Honors Theses and Study Abroad Experiences." *Preparing Tomorrow's Global Leaders: Honors International Education*. Ed. Mary Kay Mulvaney and Kim Klein. Lincoln: National Collegiate Honors Council, 2013. 217–38. NCHC Monograph Series. Print.

Osborn, Jeffrey, and Kerry Karukstis. "The Benefits of Undergraduate Research, Scholarship, and Creative Activity." *Broadening Participation in Undergraduate Research: Fostering Excellence and Enhancing the Impact*. Eds. Mary K. Boyd and Jodi L. Wesemann. Washington, D.C.: Council on Undergraduate Research, 2009. Print.

Outcalt, Charles. "The Importance of Community College Honors Programs." *New Directions for Community Colleges* 108 (1999): 59–68. Print.

Peterson, Dale. "The Start of Everything that Followed." *Amherst Magazine* (Winter 2009). Web. <https://www.amherst.edu/aboutamherst/magazine/issues/2009winter/dfw/peterson/node/97025>. [On David Foster Wallace's honors thesis, a 700-page novel that was published as *The Broom of the System.*]

Phillips, John Aristotle, and David Michaelis. *Mushroom: The True Story of the A-Bomb Kid.* New York: Morrow, 1978. Print.

Russo, Richard. *Straight Man.* New York: Random House, 1997. Print.

Sagor, Richard. *Guiding School Improvement with Action Research.* Alexandria, VA: Association for Supervision and Curriculum Development, 2000. Print.

Savage, Hallie E. Rev. of *How to Write a BA Thesis: A Practical Guide from Your First Ideas to Your Finished Paper*, by Charles Lipson. *JNCHC* 6.2 (2005): 139–40. Print.

Sederburg, Peter C., ed. *The Honors College Phenomenon.* Lincoln: National Collegiate Honors Council, NCHC Monograph Series, 2008. Print.

Stromberg, Joseph. "I Sold My Undergraduate Thesis to a Print Content Farm." *Slate* 23 Mar. 2014. Web. <http://www.slate.com/articles/technology/future_tense/2014/03/lap_lambert_academic_publishing_my_trip_to_a_print_content_farm.html>.

Wallace, David Foster. "Brief Interview with a Five Draft Man." *Amherst Magazine* (Spring 1999). Web. <https://www.amherst.edu/aboutamherst/magazine/extra/node/66410>.

Walshe, Emily. "Athena, Telemachus, and the Honors Student Odyssey: The Academic Librarian as an Agent in Mentored Learning." *JNCHC* 6.1 (2005): 85–93. Print.

Walshe, Emily C. "Conducting Research in Honors." *HIP* 6 (2010): 17–55. Print.

Wilson, Anne M., and Robert F. Holm. "The Effects on Outcomes of Financing Undergraduate Thesis Research at Butler University." *JNCHC* 8.1 (2007): 77–87. Print.

Winn, Peter. "Mentor at Princeton Recalls Sotomayor's Evolution." *The Washington Post* 12 July 2009. Web. <http://www.washingtonpost.com/wpdyn/content/article/2009/07/09/AR2009070902391.html>.

SELECTED WEBSITES

Many institutions provide thesis information on their websites. Some are minimal, but the following are, in our estimation, quite helpful. Many of them provide forms and handouts that can serve as models for other thesis programs. In addition, we suggest visiting the NCHC website <http://www.nchchonors.org>, which lists member institutions, to investigate various honors program websites worth exploring in greater depth.

Albion College
<http://www.albion.edu/academics/programs-of-distinction/honors-program/current-students/honors-and-departmental-theses>

American University
<http://www.american.edu/provost/honors/capstones.cfm>

Andrews University
<https://www.andrews.edu/services/honors/resources/advisors-handbook-thesis-proposal.pdf>

Arizona State University
<http://barretthonors.asu.edu/academics/thesis-and-creative-project>

Austin College
<http://www.austincollege.edu/academics/awards-honors/departmental-honors-program/honors-thesis-formatting>

Ball State University
<http://cms.bsu.edu/Academics/CollegesandDepartments/HonorsCollege/AcademicsandAdmissions/SeniorThesisProjectGuidelines.aspx>

Berry College
<http://www.berry.edu/academics/honors/thesis>

Brigham Young University
<http://honors.byu.edu/content/thesis-overview>

Emerson College
<http://www.emerson.edu/academics/departments/liber
al-arts-interdisciplinary-studies/honors-program/forms-re
sources>

Gateway Community College
<http://www.gatewaycc.edu/honors-program>

Greensboro College
<http://www.greensboro.edu/academics/programs/honors/
honors-thesis-info>

Kent State University
<http://www2.kent.edu/honors/seniorhonorsthesis/upload/
revised-thesis-handbook-13.pdf>

Long Island University, Post
<http://www.liu.edu/CWPost/Academics/Programs/Special/
Honors/Tutorial>

Louisiana State University
<https://www.honors.lsu.edu/current-students/academics/
curriculum/thesis>

Mary Baldwin College
<http://www.mbc.edu/honors/thesisguidelines>

Mohawk Valley Community College
<http://www.mvcc.edu/honors-program>

Saint John's University
<http://www.csbsju.edu/honors-thesis-program>

Scottsdale Community College
<http://www.scottsdalecc.edu/academics/honors-program/
honors-contract>

State University of New York at Oswego
<http://www.oswego.edu/academics/opportunities/honors/
program/thesis.html>

Syracuse University
<http://honors.syr.edu/capstone>

University of California, Riverside
<http://honors.ucr.edu/current_students/thesis>

University of Illinois at Chicago
<http://www.uic.edu/honors/learning/documents/HC%20
Handbook%202013-15.pdf>

University of Maine
<http://www.honors.umaine.edu/academics/thesis>

University of Massachusetts
<https://www.honors.umass.edu/capstone-experience>

University of South Florida, St. Petersburg
<http://www1.usfsp.edu/coas/honors/documents/Thesisin
fopacket.pdf>

University of Wyoming
<http://www.uwyo.edu/honors/senior-honors-project>

ABOUT THE AUTHORS

MARK ANDERSON was the founding director of the SUNY Brockport Honors Program. He was awarded the SUNY Chancellor's Award for Excellence in Teaching and a Blinken Administrative Fellowship for a study of honors programs, societies, and awards in SUNY. He has served as President of the Northeast Regional Honors Council and was a member of the Publications Board of the National Collegiate Honors Council. He has also worked as a Program Officer for the National Endowment for the Humanities and taught at the University of Nottingham, England; Iowa State University; the University of Maryland—Far East; and Montana State University.

KAREN LYONS is Associate Director of the University Honors Program at the University of Nebraska–Lincoln, the institution where she earned her PhD in English. She is a member of the English faculty as well as the Women's and Gender Studies faculty. Karen has been on the Publications Board of the National Collegiate Honors Council since 2000; she is currently a member of NCHC's Portz Fellowship Committee and is a past member of its Semesters Committee.

NORMAN WEINER is Distinguished Service Professor Emeritus and Honors Director Emeritus at SUNY Oswego. He was a member of the Oswego faculty for forty-two years, eighteen of them as Director of the Honors Program. He has served as a consultant to numerous institutions and honors programs. He was President of the Northeast Regional Honors Council. He was also co-chair of the Publications Board of the National Collegiate Honors Council for many years, and he also served NCHC as Conference Chair of the 2003 Annual Conference in Chicago and then as its President.

ABOUT THE NCHC MONOGRAPH SERIES

The Publications Board of the National Collegiate Honors Council typically publishes two to three monographs a year. The subject matter and style range widely: from handbooks on nuts-and-bolts practices and discussions of honors pedagogy to anthologies on diverse topics addressing honors education and issues relevant to higher education.

The Publications Board encourages people with expertise interested in writing such a monograph to submit a prospectus. Prospective authors or editors of an anthology should submit a proposal discussing the purpose or scope of the manuscript; a prospectus that includes a chapter by chapter summary; a brief writing sample, preferably a draft of the introduction or an early chapter; and a *curriculum vitae*. All monograph proposals will be reviewed by the NCHC Publications Board.

Direct all proposals, manuscripts, and inquiries about submitting a proposal to the General Editor of the Monograph Series:

Dr. Jeffrey A. Portnoy
General Editor, Monograph Series
Honors Program
Georgia Perimeter College
555 N. Indian Creek Drive
Clarkston, GA 30021-2396

jeffrey.portnoy@gpc.edu

(678) 891-3620

NCHC Monographs & Journals

Assessing and Evaluating Honors Programs and Honors Colleges: A Practical Handbook by Rosalie Otero and Robert Spurrier (2005, 98pp). This monograph includes an overview of assessment and evaluation practices and strategies. It explores the process for conducting self-studies and discusses the differences between using consultants and external reviewers. It provides a guide to conducting external reviews along with information about how to become an NCHC-Recommended Site Visitor. A dozen appendices provide examples of "best practices."

Beginning in Honors: A Handbook by Samuel Schuman (Fourth Edition, 2006, 80pp). Advice on starting a new honors program. Covers budgets, recruiting students and faculty, physical plant, administrative concerns, curriculum design, and descriptions of some model programs.

Fundrai$ing for Honor$: A Handbook by Larry R. Andrews (2009, 160pp). Offers information and advice on raising money for honors, beginning with easy first steps and progressing to more sophisticated and ambitious fundraising activities.

A Handbook for Honors Administrators by Ada Long (1995, 117pp). Everything an honors administrator needs to know, including a description of some models of honors administration.

A Handbook for Honors Programs at Two-Year Colleges by Theresa James (2006, 136pp). A useful handbook for two-year schools contemplating beginning or redesigning their honors program and for four-year schools doing likewise or wanting to increase awareness about two-year programs and articulation agreements. Contains extensive appendices about honors contracts and a comprehensive bibliography on honors education.

The Honors College Phenomenon edited by Peter C. Sederberg (2008, 172pp). This monograph examines the growth of honors colleges since 1990: historical and descriptive characterizations of the trend, alternative models that include determining whether becoming a college is appropriate, and stories of creation and recreation. Leaders whose institutions are contemplating or taking this step as well as those directing established colleges should find these essays valuable.

Honors Composition: Historical Perspectives and Contemporary Practices by Annmarie Guzy (2003, 182pp). Parallel historical developments in honors and composition studies; contemporary honors writing projects ranging from admission essays to theses as reported by over 300 NCHC members.

Honors Programs at Smaller Colleges by Samuel Schuman (Third Edition, 2011, 80pp). Practical and comprehensive advice on creating and managing honors programs with particular emphasis on colleges with fewer than 4,000 students.

The Honors Thesis: A Handbook for Honors Directors, Deans, and Faculty Advisors by Mark Anderson, Karen Lyons, and Norman Weiner (2014, 176pp). To all those who design, administer, and implement an honors thesis program, this handbook offers a range of options, models, best practices, and philosophies that illustrate how to evaluate an honors thesis program, solve pressing problems, select effective requirements and procedures, or introduce a new honors thesis program.

If Honors Students Were People: Holistic Honors Higher Education by Samuel Schuman (2013, 256pp). What if Honors students were people? What if they were not disembodied intellects but whole persons with physical bodies and questing spirits? Of course . . . they are. This monograph examines the spiritual yearnings of college students and the relationship between exercise and learning.

Inspiring Exemplary Teaching and Learning: Perspectives on Teaching Academically Talented College Students edited by Larry Clark and John Zubizarreta (2008, 216pp). This rich collection of essays offers valuable insights into innovative teaching and significant learning in the context of academically challenging classrooms and programs. The volume provides theoretical, descriptive, and practical resources, including models of effective instructional practices, examples of successful courses designed for enhanced learning, and a list of online links to teaching and learning centers and educational databases worldwide.

NCHC Monographs & Journals

The Other Culture: Science and Mathematics Education in Honors edited by Ellen B. Buckner and Keith Garbutt (2012, 296pp). A collection of essays about teaching science and math in an honors context: topics include science in society, strategies for science and non-science majors, the threat of pseudoscience, chemistry, interdisciplinary science, scientific literacy, philosophy of science, thesis development, calculus, and statistics.

Partners in the Parks: Field Guide to an Experiential Program in the National Parks by Joan Digby with reflective essays on theory and practice by student and faculty participants and National Park Service personnel (2010, 272pp). This monograph explores an experiential-learning program that fosters immersion in and stewardship of the national parks. The topics include program designs, group dynamics, philosophical and political issues, photography, wilderness exploration, and assessment.

Place as Text: Approaches to Active Learning edited by Bernice Braid and Ada Long (Second Edition, 2010, 128pp). Updated theory, information, and advice on experiential pedagogies developed within NCHC during the past 35 years, including Honors Semesters and City as Text™, along with suggested adaptations to multiple educational contexts.

Preparing Tomorrow's Global Leaders: Honors International Education edited by Mary Kay Mulvaney and Kim Klein (2013, 400pp). A valuable resource for initiating or expanding honors study abroad programs, these essays examine theoretical issues, curricular and faculty development, assessment, funding, and security. The monograph also provides models of successful programs that incorporate high-impact educational practices, including City as Text™ pedagogy, service learning, and undergraduate research.

Setting the Table for Diversity edited by Lisa L. Coleman and Jonathan D. Kotinek (2010, 288pp). This collection of essays provides definitions of diversity in honors, explores the challenges and opportunities diversity brings to honors education, and depicts the transformative nature of diversity when coupled with equity and inclusion. These essays discuss African American, Latina/o, international, and first-generation students as well as students with disabilities. Other issues include experiential and service learning, the politics of diversity, and the psychological resistance to it. Appendices relating to NCHC member institutions contain diversity statements and a structural diversity survey.

Shatter the Glassy Stare: Implementing Experiential Learning in Higher Education edited by Peter A. Machonis (2008, 160pp). A companion piece to *Place as Text*, focusing on recent, innovative applications of City as Text™ teaching strategies. Chapters on campus as text, local neighborhoods, study abroad, science courses, writing exercises, and philosophical considerations, with practical materials for instituting this pedagogy.

Teaching and Learning in Honors edited by Cheryl L. Fuiks and Larry Clark (2000, 128pp). Presents a variety of perspectives on teaching and learning useful to anyone developing new or renovating established honors curricula.

Writing on Your Feet: Reflective Practices in City as Text™ edited by Ada Long (2014, 160pp). A sequel to the NCHC monographs *Place as Text: Approaches to Active Learning* and *Shatter the Glassy Stare: Implementing Experiential Learning in Higher Education*, this volume explores the role of reflective writing in the process of active learning while also paying homage to the City as Text™ approach to experiential education that has been pioneered by Bernice Braid and sponsored by NCHC during the past four decades.

Journal of the National Collegiate Honors Council (JNCHC) is a semi-annual periodical featuring scholarly articles on honors education. Articles may include analyses of trends in teaching methodology, articles on interdisciplinary efforts, discussions of problems common to honors programs, items on the national higher education agenda, and presentations of emergent issues relevant to honors education.

Honors in Practice (HIP) is an annual journal that accommodates the need and desire for articles about nuts-and-bolts practices by featuring practical and descriptive essays on topics such as successful honors courses, suggestions for out-of-class experiences, administrative issues, and other topics of interest to honors administrators, faculty, and students.

NCHC Publication Order Form

Purchases may be made by calling 402-472-9150, emailing nchc@unl.edu, visiting our website <http://www. nchchonors.org>, or mailing a check or money order payable to: NCHC • 1100 Neihardt Residence Center • University of Nebraska–Lincoln • 540 N. 16th Street • Lincoln, NE 68588-0627.   FEIN 52–1188042

	Member	Non-Member	No. of Copies	Amount This Item
Monographs:				
Assessing and Evaluating Honors Programs and Honors Colleges: A Practical Handbook*	$25.00	$45.00		
Beginning in Honors: A Handbook (4th Ed.)	$25.00	$45.00		
Fundrai$ing for Honor$: A Handbook*	$25.00	$45.00		
A Handbook for Honors Administrators	$25.00	$45.00		
A Handbook for Honors Programs at Two-Year Colleges*	$25.00	$45.00		
The Honors College Phenomenon	$25.00	$45.00		
Honors Composition: Historical Perspectives and Contemporary Practices	$25.00	$45.00		
Honors Programs at Smaller Colleges (3rd Ed.)*	$25.00	$45.00		
The Honors Thesis: A Handbook for Honors Directors, Deans, and Faculty Advisors	$25.00	$45.00		
If Honors Students Were People: Holistic Honors Higher Education	$25.00	$45.00		
Inspiring Exemplary Teaching and Learning: Perspectives on Teaching Academically Talented College Students*	$25.00	$45.00		
The Other Culture: Science and Mathematics Education in Honors	$25.00	$45.00		
Partners in the Parks: Field Guide to an Experiential Program in the National Parks	$25.00	$45.00		
Place as Text: Approaches to Active Learning (2nd Ed.)	$25.00	$45.00		
Preparing Tomorrow's Global Leaders: Honors International Education	$25.00	$45.00		
Setting the Table for Diversity	$25.00	$45.00		
Shatter the Glassy Stare: Implementing Experiential Learning in Higher Education	$25.00	$45.00		
Teaching and Learning in Honors*	$25.00	$45.00		
Writing on Your Feet: Reflective Practices in City as Text™	$25.00	$45.00		
Journals:				
Journal of the National Collegiate Honors Council (JNCHC) Specify Vol/Issue ____/____	$25.00	$45.00		
Honors in Practice (HIP) Specify Vol ____	$25.00	$45.00		
Total Copies Ordered and Total Amount Paid:				$

Name_____ Institution _____

Address _____

City, State, Zip _____

Phone _____ Fax_____ Email _____

*Print-on-Demand publications—will be delivered in 4-6 weeks.

Shipping costs will be calculated on the number of items purchased.

Apply a 20% discount if 10+ copies are purchased.